SO-ALM-756

THE OFFICIAL
WHEEL
OF
FORTUNE
PUZZLE BOOK

THE OFFICIAL WHEEL OF FORTUNE PUZZLE BOOK

Introduction by Merv Griffin
Text by Nancy Jones

BANTAM BOOKS
TORONTO · NEW YORK · LONDON · SYDNEY · AUCKLAND

ACKNOWLEDGEMENTS

PROJECT EDITOR: Barbara Alpert
ASSISTANT: Andrea Rider

THE OFFICIAL WHEEL OF FORTUNE PUZZLE BOOK
A Bantam Book / December 1987

ISBN 0-553-27204-7

Published simultaneously in the United States and Canada

PRINTED IN THE UNITED STATES OF AMERICA

KR   0 9 8 7 6 5 4 3 2 1

THE OFFICIAL WHEEL OF FORTUNE PUZZLE BOOK

Introduction by Merv Griffin

The publication of *The Official WHEEL OF FORTUNE Puzzle Book* brings full circle the WHEEL OF FORTUNE story, and I'll tell you why. More than fifty years ago, my sister Barbara and I used to play the game "Hangman" in the backseat of the family car when we drove off on vacations or Sunday trips. We'd pass the time by trading puzzles and keeping track of our games. Lucky for me that we did.

During the many years that I spent traveling the country on a bus with Freddy Martin's band, I did more than my share of crossword puzzles. In fact, to this day, I start my mornings by working out the crossword puzzles in the newspaper. Games have always been a part of my life. I hosted a game show called *Play Your Hunch* prior to launching my career as a talk-show host. Then in 1963 I started my own company, which operated out of the dining room of my New York apartment. I enlisted the aid of relatives and friends to try out new games, one of which turned out to be *Jeopardy*. Well, *Jeopardy* turned out to be a smash hit and I found myself in the game-show business in a big way.

I began tinkering with the idea of using "Hangman" in a game show. An idea for a game show starts as simply as that. The next step is to try and find a framework to make that basic idea a real "game," one that the audience at home will enjoy playing, and one that builds to a climax, or "bonus" round. That process can take months or years. The idea for using a "Wheel of Fortune" for a "Hangman" came to me one evening in Las Vegas, where I was appearing with my show. I was watching a pack of gamblers eagerly watching this wheel spin, and I knew it was worth a try. When we injected the additional element of "shopping" for prizes—the original name of the show was, in fact, *Shopper's Bazaar*— we knew we had the makings of the kind of show that home viewers could be involved with on many levels.

The show launched on NBC in 1974, and we all quickly learned that I wasn't the only one in America who still loved to play "Hangman." The show jumped to the top of the ratings and has performed terrifically ever since. In 1983 the nighttime version of WHEEL OF FORTUNE was introduced, and the show found an even larger audience, to the point where now the show is watched by more than forty-two million viewers per day.

And I'll tell you what, I still watch it. Every day. Even though I have an extremely competent production staff, I check in to see that all of the elements of the game are working as I want them to. And I love to see which puzzles the contestants wrestle with and which ones they solve easily. I always keep a pad of paper and pen handy to write new puzzles when I think of them, or more often than not, someone says something that will make a puzzle. I occasionally drive my staff nuts by stopping them in midsentence to write down a phrase they've used that will make a good WHEEL OF FORTUNE puzzle.

Now we've got this puzzle book, so "Wheelies" and puzzle fans can play the game wherever they go. I hope you have as much fun matching wits with these puzzles as we do bringing them to you. Good playing!

PEOPLE, PUZZLES, AND PRIZES

How are game shows born, and who creates them? Literally hundreds of new game shows are presented to broadcasting executives each year. Of these, only a handful ever make it on the air, and only a few of those "catch" and become hits. What makes a game show a hit? Is there a "formula" for a successful game show?

There are several answers to each of these questions, depending on whom you ask. But one of the keys to creating successful game shows seems to have something to do with enjoying playing the game . . . a pleasure that in some cases goes all the way back to childhood. For Merv Griffin, a favorite kids' game such as "Hangman" became more than a pleasant memory. Reshaped and rethought, as WHEEL OF FORTUNE, it has evolved into the top-rated television game show in America!

The program originally aired back in the 1974–75 season, in a daytime version on NBC, and added a nighttime version in September 1983. Current hosts Pat Sajak and Vanna White have achieved national acclaim for their roles in the show's current success, but how many people can answer this trivia question— Who were the original host and hostess of WHEEL OF FORTUNE? Time's up. Answer: Chuck Woolery (most recently host of *The Love Connection*) and the lovely Susan Stafford.

The half-hour episodes of WHEEL OF FORTUNE are produced in Burbank, California—five shows filmed on a single taping day! How is it done so that it looks so easy? Well, there are dozens of talented people behind the scenes who put the show together, including Nancy Jones, the only woman producer in the television game-show business, and Merv Griffin himself, who still creates puzzles for the program. Then, of course, there are Pat and Vanna, the on-screen hosts who give the show its pace and personality! Here are some brief "up close and personal" biographies of these fabulous four—what they do, how they came to be part of WHEEL OF FORTUNE, and how they feel about what they do!

Producer Nancy Jones:

When asked how she'd define her role as producer of WHEEL OF FORTUNE, Nancy Jones smiled and replied, "Jack-of-all-trades. We not only produce a TV show, we run a department store. Last year, we gave away over $2 million in prizes, and even though we have a prize agency that helps to administer that, we still have to deal with a tremendous amount of paperwork, the logistics of getting new merchandise and getting the old merchandise shipped out to contestants. That's a big part of my function. I buy a lot of the prizes. I write a lot of copy describing each of the fabulous prizes on the show and arrange all of the prize showcases. I work on puzzles with Merv Griffin. I work in the contestant area, too, and I go on promotional tours to publicize the show. I'd describe my job as combining management with creative skills and artistic taste—a great combination that adds up to a job I love."

Merv Griffin:

In her role as producer of this number-one-rated show, Nancy is perhaps best qualified to tell the public about her boss, Merv Griffin. When asked to describe the man who, in addition to WHEEL OF FORTUNE, also created the supersuccessful game show *Jeopardy*, Nancy spoke with enthusiasm. "Merv is a very interesting man. First, he's a self-made millionaire, and just as nice as he seems on television. He loves to travel. He has his own jet and on the spur of the moment may decide to fly to Rio or Paris or to Palm Beach. He's been dating Eva Gabor, but I don't know if marriage plans are in his future. Ask him!

"Now that Merv no longer hosts his daily talk show, he has much more time to devote to business and to running Merv Griffin Enterprises, which produces *Jeopardy* and *Dance Fever* in addition to WHEEL OF FORTUNE, and has a number of exciting projects in development, including a WHEEL OF FORTUNE movie. Merv's office is full of gorgeous green plants that flourish in the southern California sunlight, and the walls are covered with photographs of Merv and the many internationally famous people he has known. Most meetings take place around a large black glass coffee table, with the participants sitting on big, overstuffed, comfortable sofas.

"Merv's style is informal and relaxed. He frequently comes to the office in a warm-up suit or in jeans and sneakers. But he runs a tight ship. He knows everything that's going on. He has a memory like an elephant and he watches WHEEL OF FORTUNE every day."

Pat Sajak:

"It's really a balancing act for me out there," host Pat Sajak says, summing up *his* job on WHEEL OF FORTUNE. "I think you have to have some kind of sense of humor and keep the show light. It is, after all, only a game show." Pat is in his sixth year as host, having joined the show in December 1981. Born and raised in Chicago, he began his career as a newscaster and later worked as a disc jockey for the U.S. Army radio station in Saigon. He's had a number of jobs in television, including weatherman in both Nashville and Los Angeles, as well as stints doing public affairs broadcasting and a "drivetime" radio program. In addition to his visible role on WHEEL OF FORTUNE, Pat made his feature-film debut in *Airplane II—The Sequel* and has become a regular host of the nationally broadcast "Macy's Thanksgiving Day Parade" on NBC.

Nancy Jones adds, "Pat is just like he is on the show. He's very easygoing, with a great sense of humor. He's smart and dependable. He keeps his private life very private. After working with him for six years, here's what I know about Pat: He's from Chicago, and he's a big baseball fan—the Cubs, of course. He likes brunettes. He loves chocolate. He likes to eat in good restaurants and go to the movies. He's an avid reader, interested in politics and world affairs. He plays racquetball and he drives a big old gray Ford." And cohost Vanna White calls Pat "witty, professional, fun to work with . . . a real person. He's having a good time, and that's why we get along so well. I trust him, and we're good friends. We've never gotten into an argument. And he's cute."

Vanna White:

Hostess Vanna White describes herself as "a cheerleader. I try to give the players inspiration. I think it's important that every player we have on the show, whether a winner or loser, still has a great time." Born in North Myrtle Beach, South Carolina, Vanna left home after high school to attend the Atlanta School of Fashion Design in Atlanta, Georgia, where she became one of that city's top fashion models. In 1980, Vanna decided to move to Los Angeles to pursue a lifelong dream—an acting career. In 1982, after playing roles in such feature films as *Looker* and *Graduation Day*, Vanna beat out over two hundred other hopefuls to win her current job on WHEEL OF FORTUNE. Producer Nancy Jones points out that Vanna's role has greatly contributed to the show's phenomenal ratings success. "We thought it was time to have a more prominent role for a woman on a game show—other than just as a model. We wanted someone who had some personality—someone who could reach out to the audience. Vanna has succeeded in doing just that." Nancy adds that Vanna "loves being famous and really appreciates her fans. She enjoys tooling around town in her new white Mercedes 450SL. When she's not taping WHEEL OF FORTUNE, she's busy doing commercials or traveling somewhere for a personal appearance. Success hasn't changed her—she's still the sweet, cooperative girl-next-door." Pat Sajak agrees, adding, "Vanna is as unaffected by success as anyone I've ever seen. And that's really surprising, because she had limited success before this, and oftentimes that can really turn your head. But she's handled it beautifully and gracefully."

The Puzzles

The puzzles are at the heart of the WHEEL OF FORTUNE show. Nancy Jones describes it as "Merv's pet area." Suggestions for puzzles may come from anyone on the staff of the program. (Even Pat and Vanna have handed in lists of suggested puzzles.) Merv thinks up many of the toughest WHEEL OF FORTUNE puzzles himself. Producer Nancy Jones outlines the process: "We meet around the large glass coffee table in Merv's office to decide which puzzles will be grouped together—we're always on the lookout for interesting letter combinations. The puzzles then go to our research department for meticulous checking of spelling and category. Then our crack researchers have to arrange the words to fit our WHEEL OF FORTUNE puzzle board.

"Puzzles are always kept top secret until just before the show, when at the last minute they are chosen by the representative from the network's Compliance and Practices department."

A reminder: all of the puzzles in The Official WHEEL OF FORTUNE Puzzle Book were created by the same people who create and choose the puzzles for the show itself!

The Prizes

The show's producer, Nancy Jones, is also responsible for the array of valuable prizes contestants "buy" with the money they win by solving the WHEEL puzzles. "It's fabulous merchandise!" Nancy reports. "It's as if I'm managing an entire department store—only instead of selling merchandise, we're giving it away to the smart and lucky WHEEL OF FORTUNE winners. If you've seen the show, you know we have everything from soup to nuts. We've given away ceramic pigs, microwave ovens, hand-carved furniture, and everything in between and beyond, up to the most glamorous furs and jewels in the world.

"Our staff works to secure the most luxurious furniture, the trendiest automobiles, the most exotic trips, and the most advanced electronics equipment on the market today. A lot of shopping is done on magnificent Rodeo Drive in Beverly Hills, in some of the finest, most exclusive stores in the country. We're always looking for something new and different. Once we select the merchandise, it has to be delivered to the studio, copy must be written to describe it, it has to be scheduled to appear on particular shows, awarded to contestants, and then shipped to their homes.

"We give away several million dollars in prizes each year on WHEEL OF FORTUNE, so this is a vast inventory-control operation unto itself. On every show we offer prizes totaling from $90,000 to $150,000, and we usually give away at least $15,000 to $20,000 per show, among the three contestants."

When Pat Sajak was asked about some of his favorite prizes, he answered, "I'm a big fan of the offbeat prizes. Whenever we go on promotional trips, people always ask us about the ceramic dogs and all. They're not just putting us on. That stuff's become part of the show. We have people who are disappointed when there's not a ceramic animal on our show to play for. I think Mr. Meatsmoker™ is great, and other things I can play and have a little fun with."

One little-known fact that fans of the show may not have realized—the large gold stars displayed next to certain items in the prize showcases signify that those prizes may be played for by contestants who reach the bonus round.

The most popular prizes on the show: cars!

And yes, contestants do have to report any prizes won on their income tax returns and pay taxes on them. Prizes may not be exchanged for cash, but contestants do have the option of deciding, once the show is over, not to accept certain prizes (for tax or other reasons).

HOW TO PLAY
THE OFFICIAL WHEEL OF
FORTUNE PUZZLE BOOK

- At the top of each page, note the category for the puzzle.

- We've given you a few letters to help you figure out the answer. If you can solve it on the basis of these clues, you get a perfect score of 100 points.

- If you need to buy a vowel, it costs you 10 points; a consonant 5 points. Use the letter board on each page to tally up the letters you've requested, then subtract the points from 100 to get your final score.

- *To buy a vowel or consonant:* Turn to the alphabetical pages in the back of the book and look up the letter you've chosen. Find the puzzle number in the listing, and you'll see how many of that letter are in the puzzle, and in which numbered spaces they belong. Write them in, then try again to guess the puzzle. Continue buying letters until you've found the answer.

Scoring Chart

100 points—Perfect! Merv would be proud of you.
85–95—Very good! Vanna thinks you're terrific.
70–80—Good try! Pat is rooting for you to win.
Under 70—Practice, practice, practice! You can do better next time!

LEVEL I

CATEGORY: **PHRASE**

PUZZLE NUMBER: **1**

A	L	E	G	E	N	D	N
1	2	3	4	5	6	7	8	9

H	I	S		O	W	N	T	I	T	W
10	11	12	13	14	15	16	17	18	9

POINTS: 100 for no letters added.
Subtract 5 points for each consonant guessed.
Subtract 10 points for each vowel guessed.

TOTAL: _____

USED LETTER BOARD: E A R O I N __ __ __

10

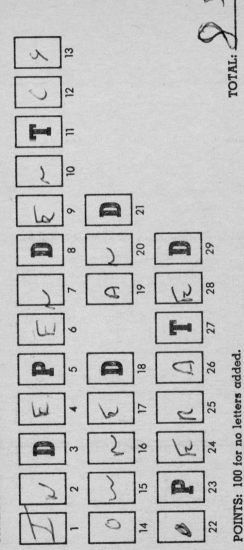

TOTAL: _____

POINTS: 100 for no letters added.
   Subtract 5 points for each consonant guessed.
   Subtract 10 points for each vowel guessed.

USED LETTER BOARD: _____

CATEGORY: **THINGS**

PUZZLE NUMBER: **3**

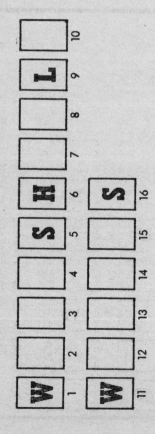

W				S	H			L	
1	2	3	4	5	6	7	8	9	10

W					S
11	12	13	14	15	16

POINTS: 100 for no letters added.
Subtract 5 points for each consonant guessed.
Subtract 10 points for each vowel guessed.

TOTAL: _____

USED LETTER BOARD: _____ _____ _____ _____

12

CATEGORY: PERSON

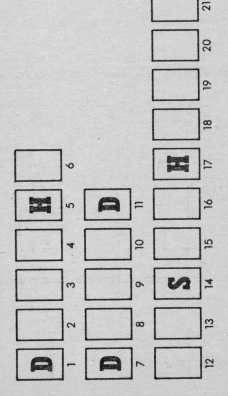

D				H	
1	2	3	4	5	6

D				D	
7	8	9	10	11	

	S			H
12	13	14	15	16	17

18	19	20	21

POINTS: 100 for no letters added.
Subtract 5 points for each consonant guessed.
Subtract 10 points for each vowel guessed.

TOTAL: _____

USED LETTER BOARD: _____ _____ _____ _____

13

CATEGORY: **PHRASE**

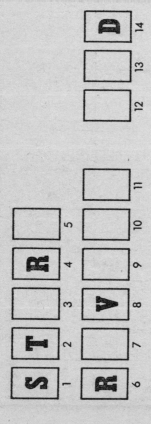

S	T		R	
1	2	3	4	5

R		V			
6	7	8	9	10	11

		D
12	13	14

POINTS: 100 for no letters added.
  Subtract 5 points for each consonant guessed.
  Subtract 10 points for each vowel guessed.

TOTAL: _____

USED LETTER BOARD: — — — — —

14

CATEGORY: **PERSON** PUZZLE NUMBER: **6**

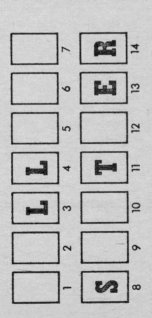

1	2	3	4	5	6	7
		L	L			

8	9	10	11	12	13	14
S			T		E	R

POINTS: 100 for no letters added.
Subtract 5 points for each consonant guessed.
Subtract 10 points for each vowel guessed.

TOTAL: ________

USED LETTER BOARD: ___ ___ ___ ___ ___ ___ ___ ___

CATEGORY: **THING**

PUZZLE NUMBER: **7**

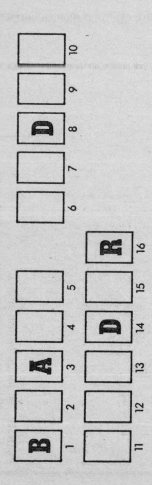

B		A		
1	2	3	4	5

	D		
6	7	8	9	10

			D	
11	12	13	14	15

R
16

POINTS: 100 for no letters added.
 Subtract 5 points for each consonant guessed.
 Subtract 10 points for each vowel guessed.

TOTAL: _____

USED LETTER BOARD: — — — —

16

CATEGORY: PERSON

PUZZLE NUMBER: 8

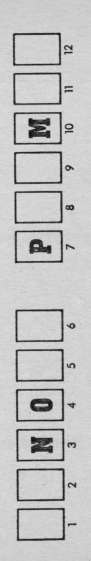

		N	O			P			M		
1	2	3	4	5	6	7	8	9	10	11	12

POINTS: 100 for no letters added.
Subtract 5 points for each consonant guessed.
Subtract 10 points for each vowel guessed.

TOTAL: _____

USED LETTER BOARD: ___ ___ ___ ___ ___

17

CATEGORY: PLACE

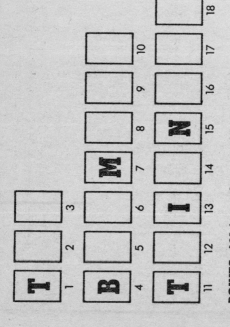

T		
1	2	3

B		
4	5	6

| M | | |
| 7 | 8 | 9 |

| | |
| 10 |

| T | I | |
| 11 | 12 | 13 |

| | N | |
| 14 | 15 | |

| | | |
| 16 | 17 | 18 |

POINTS: 100 for no letters added.
  Subtract 5 points for each consonant guessed.
  Subtract 10 points for each vowel guessed.

TOTAL: _____

USED LETTER BOARD: _ _ _ _ _ _

18

CATEGORY: PLACE

PUZZLE NUMBER: 10

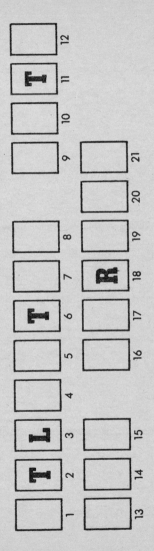

| 1 | T (2) | L (3) | 4 | 5 | T (6) | 7 | 8 | 9 | 10 | T (11) | 12 |

| 13 | 14 | 15 | 16 | 17 | R (18) | 19 | 20 | 21 |

POINTS: 100 for no letters added.
Subtract 5 points for each consonant guessed.
Subtract 10 points for each vowel guessed.

TOTAL: _____

USED LETTER BOARD: __ __ __ __ __ __ __

19

CATEGORY: FICTIONAL CHARACTERS

PUZZLE NUMBER: 11

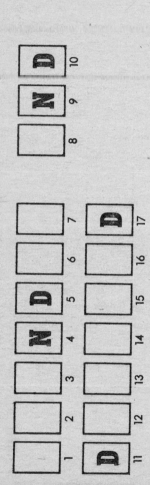

| 1 | 2 | 3 | N 4 | D 5 | 6 | 7 |

| 8 | N 9 | D 10 |

| D 11 | 12 | 13 | 14 | 15 | 16 | D 17 |

POINTS: 100 for no letters added.
Subtract 5 points for each consonant guessed.
Subtract 10 points for each vowel guessed.

TOTAL: _____

USED LETTER BOARD: ___ ___ ___ ___ ___ ___

20

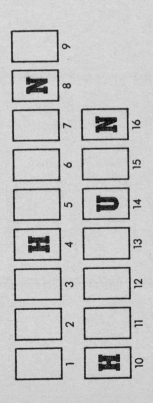

CATEGORY: PERSON

PUZZLE NUMBER: 12

| | 1 | | 2 | | 3 | **H** | 4 | | 5 | | 6 | | 7 | **N** | 8 | | 9 |

| | 10 **H** | 11 | 12 | 13 | **U** 14 | 15 | **N** 16 |

POINTS: 100 for no letters added.
Subtract 5 points for each consonant guessed.
Subtract 10 points for each vowel guessed.

TOTAL: _____

USED LETTER BOARD: _____

21

CATEGORY: **FICTIONAL CHARACTERS**

PUZZLE NUMBER: **13**

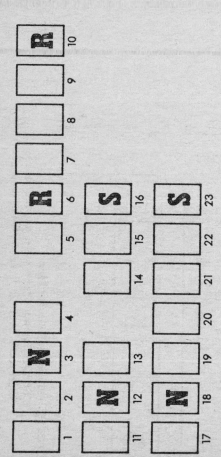

		N			R				R
1	2	3	4	5	6	7	8	9	10

	N				S		
11	12	13	14	15	16		

	N				S
17	18	19	20	21	22	23

POINTS: 100 for no letters added.
Subtract 5 points for each consonant guessed.
Subtract 10 points for each vowel guessed.

TOTAL: _____

USED LETTER BOARD: _____ _____ _____ _____

22

CATEGORY: PERSON

PUZZLE NUMBER: 14

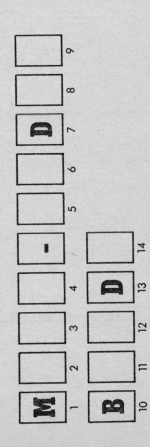

M				-		D		
1	2	3	4	5	6	7	8	9

B			D	
10	11	12	13	14

POINTS: 100 for no letters added.
Subtract 5 points for each consonant guessed.
Subtract 10 points for each vowel guessed.

TOTAL: _____

USED LETTER BOARD: _ _ _ _ _

23

CATEGORY: **THING**

PUZZLE NUMBER: **15**

TOTAL: _____

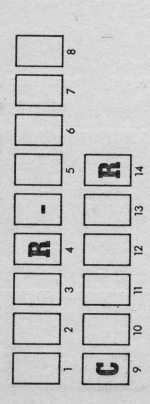

POINTS: 100 for no letters added.
Subtract 5 points for each consonant guessed.
Subtract 10 points for each vowel guessed.

USED LETTER BOARD: ___ ___ ___ ___

24

CATEGORY: **PHRASE**

PUZZLE NUMBER: **16**

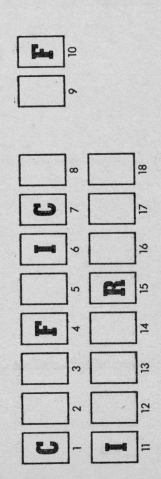

C			F		I	C				F
1	2	3	4	5	6	7	8	9		10

I				R				
11	12	13	14	15	16	17	18

POINTS: 100 for no letters added.
Subtract 5 points for each consonant guessed.
Subtract 10 points for each vowel guessed.

TOTAL: _____

USED LETTER BOARD: ___ ___ ___ ___ ___

25

CATEGORY: **THING**

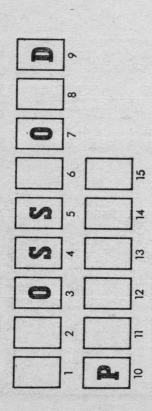

		O	S	S		O		D
1	2	3	4	5	6	7	8	9

P				
10	11	12	13	14	15

TOTAL: _____

POINTS: 100 for no letters added.
Subtract 5 points for each consonant guessed.
Subtract 10 points for each vowel guessed.

USED LETTER BOARD: ___ ___ ___ ___ ___

26

CATEGORY: QUOTATION

PUZZLE NUMBER: 18

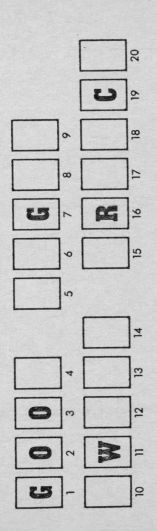

G	O	O				G		
1	2	3	4	5	6	7	8	9

	W								R			C	
10	11	12	13	14	15	16	17	18	19	20

POINTS: 100 for no letters added.
Subtract 5 points for each consonant guessed.
Subtract 10 points for each vowel guessed.

TOTAL: _____

USED LETTER BOARD: ___ ___ ___ ___

27

CATEGORY: **PHRASE**

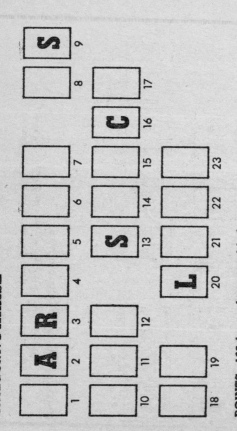

| 1 | A (2) | R (3) | 4 | 5 | 6 | 7 | 8 | S (9) |

POINTS: 100 for no letters added.
Subtract 5 points for each consonant guessed.
Subtract 10 points for each vowel guessed.

TOTAL: _____

USED LETTER BOARD: ___ ___ ___ ___

28

CATEGORY: PHRASE

PUZZLE NUMBER: **20**

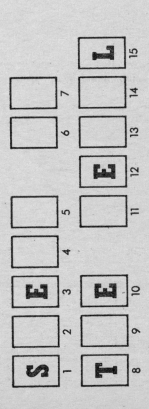

| S | | E | | | | |
|1|2|3|4|5|6|7|

| T | | E | | E | | L |
|8|9|10|11|12|13|14|15|

POINTS: 100 for no letters added.
Subtract 5 points for each consonant guessed.
Subtract 10 points for each vowel guessed.

TOTAL: _____

USED LETTER BOARD: ___ ___ ___ ___ ___ ___

29

CATEGORY: OCCUPATION

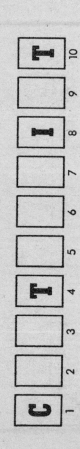

C			T				I		T
1	2	3	4	5	6	7	8	9	10

POINTS: 100 for no letters added.
    Subtract 5 points for each consonant guessed.
    Subtract 10 points for each vowel guessed.

USED LETTER BOARD: _____ _ _

TOTAL: _____

36

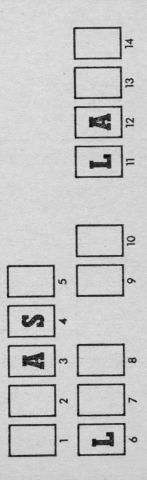

POINTS: 100 for no letters added.
Subtract 5 points for each consonant guessed.
Subtract 10 points for each vowel guessed.

TOTAL: _____

USED LETTER BOARD: — — — — — — —

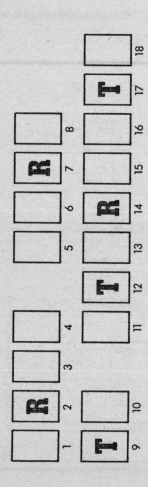

CATEGORY: **TITLE**

PUZZLE NUMBER: **23**

POINTS: 100 for no letters added.
Subtract 5 points for each consonant guessed.
Subtract 10 points for each vowel guessed.

TOTAL: _____

USED LETTER BOARD: _____

32

CATEGORY: **PHRASE**

PUZZLE NUMBER: **24**

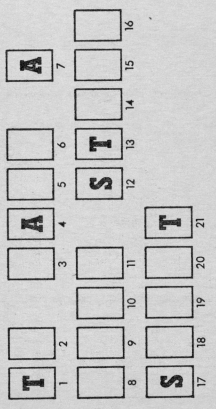

T			**A**			**A**
1	2	3	4	5	6	7

					S	**T**		
8	9	10	11	12	13	14	15	16

S				**T**
17	18	19	20	21

POINTS: 100 for no letters added.
    Subtract 5 points for each consonant guessed.
    Subtract 10 points for each vowel guessed.

TOTAL: _____

USED LETTER BOARD: —— —— —— —— —— ——

33

CATEGORY: **FICTIONAL CHARACTER**

PUZZLE NUMBER: **25**

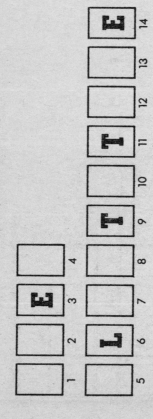

		E	
1	2	3	4

	L		T				E
5	6	7	8	9	10	11	12	13	14

POINTS: 100 for no letters added.
Subtract 5 points for each consonant guessed.
Subtract 10 points for each vowel guessed.

USED LETTER BOARD: ___ ___ ___

TOTAL: _____

34

PUZZLE NUMBER: **26**

CATEGORY: **TITLE**

						R	-
1	2	3	4	5	6	7	

	P			G	L		
8	9	10	11	12	13	14	15

		R		
16	17	18	19	20	21

POINTS: 100 for no letters added.
Subtract 5 points for each consonant guessed.
Subtract 10 points for each vowel guessed.

TOTAL: _____

USED LETTER BOARD: — — — —

35

CATEGORY: **EVENT**

PUZZLE NUMBER: **27**

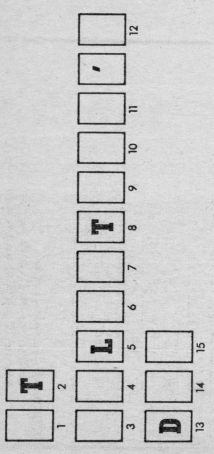

	T			L			T				
1	2	3	4	5	6	7	8	9	10	11	12

D		
13	14	15

POINTS: 100 for no letters added.
Subtract 5 points for each consonant guessed.
Subtract 10 points for each vowel guessed.

TOTAL: _____

USED LETTER BOARD: ___ ___ ___ ___ ___

36

CATEGORY: **PHRASE**

PUZZLE NUMBER: **28**

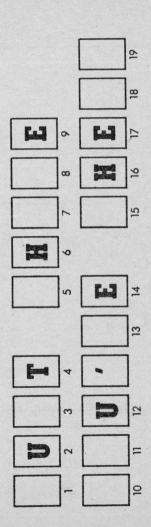

| | U | | T | |
|1|2|3|4|5|

| | H | | E |
|6|7|8|9|

| | | U | |
|10|11|12|13|

| E | | H | E |
|14|15|16|17|

| | |
|18|19|

POINTS: 100 for no letters added.
Subtract 5 points for each consonant guessed.
Subtract 10 points for each vowel guessed.

TOTAL: _____

USED LETTER BOARD: _____ _____

37

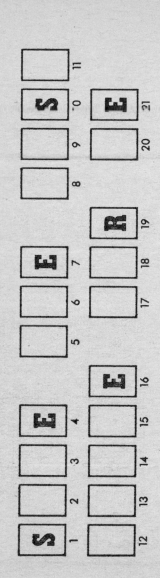

S			E			E			S	
1	2	3	4	5	6	7	8	9	10	11

				E		R		E		E
12	13	14	15	16	17	18	19	20	21

POINTS: 100 for no letters added.
Subtract 5 points for each consonant guessed.
Subtract 10 points for each vowel guessed.

TOTAL: _____

USED LETTER BOARD: ___ ___ ___

38

CATEGORY: **PHRASE**

PUZZLE NUMBER: **30**

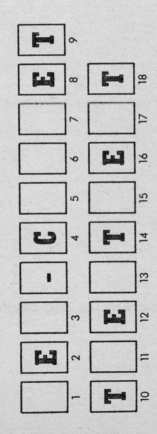

T	E		_	C			E	T
1	2	3	4	5	6	7	8	9

T	E	E	T		E		T	
10	11	12	13	14	15	16	17	18

POINTS: 100 for no letters added.
   Subtract 5 points for each consonant guessed.
   Subtract 10 points for each vowel guessed.

TOTAL: _____

USED LETTER BOARD: __ __ __ __ __ __

39

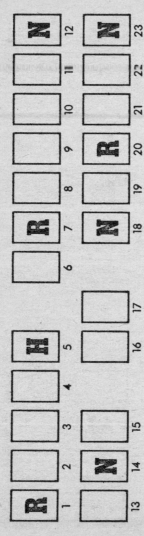

CATEGORY: FICTIONAL CHARACTERS

PUZZLE NUMBER: 31

| R | | | | H | | R | | | | | N |
|1|2|3|4|5|6|7|8|9|10|11|12|

| | N | | | | | N | | R | | | N |
|13|14|15|16|17|18|19|20|21|22|23|

POINTS: 100 for no letters added.
Subtract 5 points for each consonant guessed.
Subtract 10 points for each vowel guessed.

TOTAL: _____

USED LETTER BOARD:

40

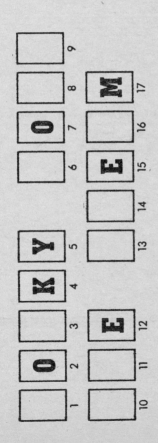

CATEGORY: **THING**

PUZZLE NUMBER: **32**

TOTAL: _____

POINTS: 100 for no letters added.
Subtract 5 points for each consonant guessed.
Subtract 10 points for each vowel guessed.

USED LETTER BOARD: — — — — — — —

41

CATEGORY: **THING**

PUZZLE NUMBER: **33**

| 1 | 2 | **F** 3 | 4 |

| 5 | 6 | **R** 7 | 8 | 9 | **F** 10 | 11 | 12 | 13 | 14 | 15 |

POINTS: 100 for no letters added.
Subtract 5 points for each consonant guessed.
Subtract 10 points for each vowel guessed.

TOTAL: _____

USED LETTER BOARD: ___ ___ ___ ___ ___

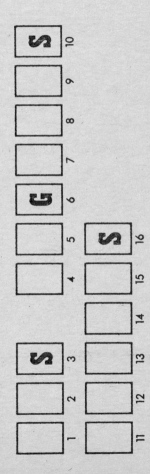

S		S			G				S
1	2	3	4	5	6	7	8	9	10

					S
11	12	13	14	15	16

TOTAL: _____

POINTS: 100 for no letters added.
  Subtract 5 points for each consonant guessed.
  Subtract 10 points for each vowel guessed.

USED LETTER BOARD: ___ ___ ___ ___ ___ ___

43

CATEGORY: THINGS

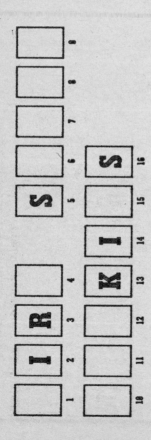

PUZZLE NUMBER: 35

POINTS: 100 for no letters added.
Subtract 5 points for each consonant guessed.
Subtract 10 points for each vowel guessed.

TOTAL: _____

USED LETTER BOARD: — — — — — — —

44

CATEGORY: OCCUPATION

PUZZLE NUMBER: 36

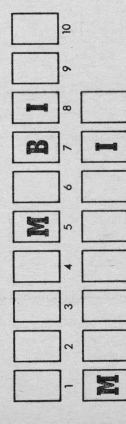

					M	B	I		
1	2	3	4	5	6	7	8	9	10

M						I		
11	12	13	14	15	16	17	18

POINTS: 100 for no letters added.
Subtract 5 points for each consonamt guessed.
Subtract 10 points for each vowel guessed.

TOTAL: _____

USED LETTER BOARD: _ _ _ _ _

45

CATEGORY: **OCCUPATION**

PUZZLE NUMBER: **37**

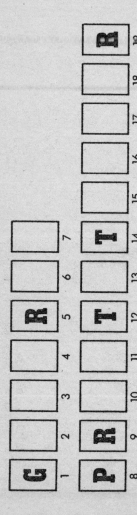

G				R		
1	2	3	4	5	6	7

P	R			T		T					R
8	9	10	11	12	13	14	15	16	17	18	19

POINTS: 100 for no letters added.
Subtract 5 points for each consonant guessed.
Subtract 10 points for each vowel guessed.

TOTAL: _____

USED LETTER BOARD: ___ ___ ___ ___ ___

46

CATEGORY: **THING**

PUZZLE NUMBER: **38**

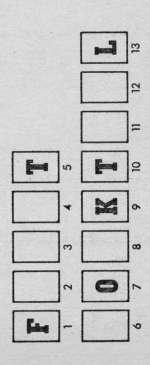

F				T
1	2	3	4	5

	O		K	T			L
6	7	8	9	10	11	12	13

POINTS: 100 for no letters added.
Subtract 5 points for each consonant guessed.
Subtract 10 points for each vowel guessed.

TOTAL: _____

USED LETTER BOARD: ___ ___ ___

47

CATEGORY: PEOPLE

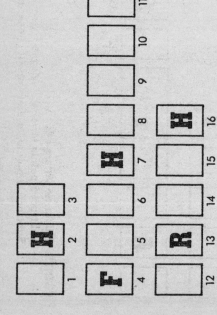

| | H | | |
| 1 | 2 | 3 | |

| F | | | | H | | |
| 4 | 5 | 6 | 7 | 8 | 9 | 10 | 11 |

| | R | | | | H |
| 12 | 13 | 14 | 15 | 16 |

POINTS: 100 for no letters added.
Subtract 5 points for each consonant guessed.
Subtract 10 points for each vowel guessed.

TOTAL: _____

USED LETTER BOARD: __ __ __ __ __ __ __

48

CATEGORY: **PHRASE**   PUZZLE NUMBER: **40**

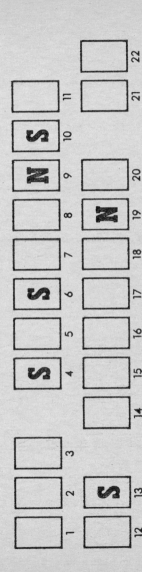

| | | |
|1|2|3|

| S | | S | | S | | | N | S | | |
|4|5|6|7|8|9|10|11|

| S | | | | | N | | |
|12|13|14|15|16|17|18|19|20|21|22|

POINTS: 100 for no letters added.
Subtract 5 points for each consonant guessed.
Subtract 10 points for each vowel guessed.

TOTAL: _____

USED LETTER BOARD: _____ _____ _____ _____

49

CATEGORY: THINGS

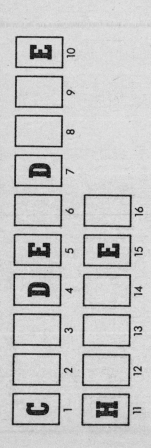

C			D	E		D			E
1	2	3	4	5	6	7	8	9	10

H				E	
11	12	13	14	15	16

POINTS: 100 for no letters added.
Subtract 5 points for each consonant guessed.
Subtract 10 points for each vowel guessed.

TOTAL: _____

USED LETTER BOARD: ___ ___ ___ ___ ___ ___

50

CATEGORY: **PHRASE**

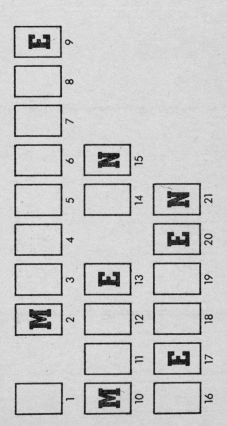

| | M | | | | | | | E |
|1|2|3|4|5|6|7|8|9|

| M | | E | | | N |
|10|11|12|13|14|15|

| | E | | | E | N |
|16|17|18|19|20|21|

POINTS: 100 for no letters added.
Subtract 5 points for each consonant guessed.
Subtract 10 points for each vowel guessed.

TOTAL: _____

USED LETTER BOARD: ___ ___ ___ ___ ___

51

CATEGORY: PEOPLE

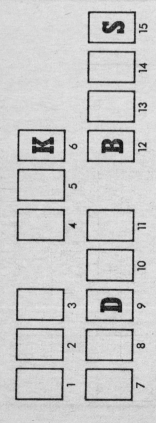

POINTS: 100 for no letters added.
Subtract 5 points for each consonant guessed.
Subtract 10 points for each vowel guessed.

TOTAL: _____

USED LETTER BOARD: _ _ _ _ _ _ _ _ _

CATEGORY: **THING**

PUZZLE NUMBER: **44**

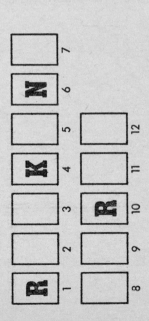

R			K		N	
1	2	3	4	5	6	7

		R			
8	9	10	11	12	

POINTS: 100 for no letters added.
Subtract 5 points for each consonant guessed.
Subtract 10 points for each vowel guessed.

TOTAL: _____

USED LETTER BOARD: ___ ___ ___ ___ ___

53

CATEGORY: **PERSON**

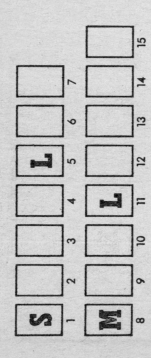

S				L		
1	2	3	4	5	6	7

M			L			
8	9	10	11	12	13	14	15

POINTS: 100 for no letters added.
Subtract 5 points for each consonant guessed.
Subtract 10 points for each vowel guessed.

TOTAL: _____

USED LETTER BOARD: ___ ___ ___ ___

54

CATEGORY: **QUOTATION**

PUZZLE NUMBER: **46**

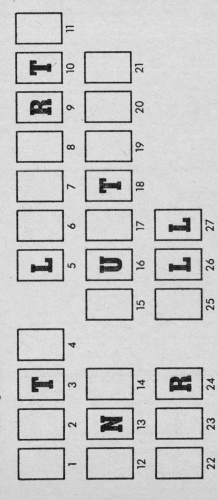

	T			L				R	T	
1	2	3	4	5	6	7	8	9	10	11

	N			U		T			
12	13	14	15	16	17	18	19	20	21

		R			L	L
22	23	24	25	26	27

POINTS: 100 for no letters added.
Subtract 5 points for each consonant guessed.
Subtract 10 points for each vowel guessed.

TOTAL: _____

USED LETTER BOARD: —— —— —— —— —— ——

55

CATEGORY: **TITLE**

PUZZLE NUMBER: **47**

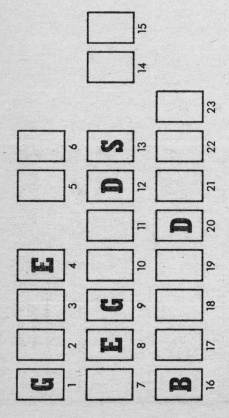

G			E			
1	2	3	4	5	6	

	E	G			D	S
7	8	9	10	11	12	13

| | | | | | | 14 | 15 |

B				D			
16	17	18	19	20	21	22	23

POINTS: 100 for no letters added.
Subtract 5 points for each consonant guessed.
Subtract 10 points for each vowel guessed.

USED LETTER BOARD: _____

TOTAL: _____

56

CATEGORY: **PHRASE**

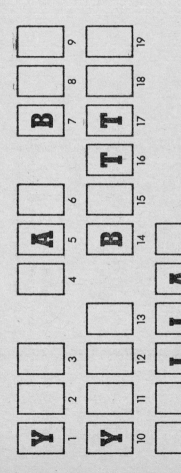

Y				Y		A			B		
1	2	3	4	5	6	7	8	9			

Y		L		B		T	T		
10	11	12	13	14	15	16	17	18	19

			L	L	A	
20	21	22	23	24	25	

POINTS: 100 for no letters added.
  Subtract 5 points for each consonant guessed.
  Subtract 10 points for each vowel guessed.

USED LETTER BOARD: _____

TOTAL: _____

57

CATEGORY: **PHRASE**

PUZZLE NUMBER: **49**

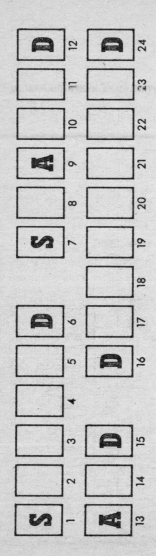

S					D		S		A			D
1	2	3	4	5	6	7	8	9	10	11	12

A		D			D						D
13	14	15	16	17	18	19	20	21	22	23	24

TOTAL: _____

POINTS: 100 for no letters added.
Subtract 5 points for each consonant guessed.
Subtract 10 points for each vowel guessed.

USED LETTER BOARD: ___ ___ ___ ___ ___

58

CATEGORY: **THINGS**

PUZZLE NUMBER: **50**

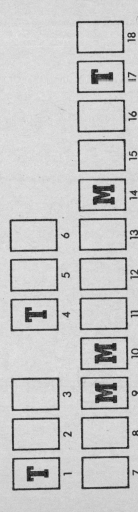

T			T		
1	2	3	4	5	6

	M	M	T				M			T	
7	8	9	10	11	12	13	14	15	16	17	18

POINTS: 100 for no letters added.
Subtract 5 points for each consonant guessed.
Subtract 10 points for each vowel guessed.

TOTAL: _____

USED LETTER BOARD: —— —— —— —— ——

59

PLAYING WHEEL
OF FORTUNE FOR REAL:
BECOMING A CONTESTANT

I t's the dream of nearly every television game-show viewer—a chance to appear on the show, win the game, and drive home in a brand-new car! For many of the viewers of WHEEL OF FORTUNE, it may remain only a wonderful fantasy, but for others, it can become a thrilling reality.

Are you eligible to be a contestant on the top-rated television game show? The rules say you must not have appeared on another game show within the past year, and that you may appear on no more than three game shows in a lifetime. Okay so far?

You must be at least eighteen years old (except for specialty weeks, when younger contestants may play the game), may not be a member of one of the performers' unions—Actor's Equity, SAG, AFTRA—and may not be a candidate for political office. Still in the running?

Good. You are required to pay your own expenses to appear on the show—airline tickets, hotel, meals, and so on. If you are planning to be in the Los Angeles area and want to try out, write to the show and make an appointment to be interviewed and tested during your visit.

Okay. You've practiced playing the home game, had friends test you, done dozens of crossword puzzles. You've gathered your courage, put on your best smile, and feel full of energy and ready to dazzle the contestant coordinators! Give it your best shot and enjoy yourself—that's what it's all about.

Producer Nancy Jones describes a typical day

in the life of a prospective WHEEL OF FORTUNE contestant:

"It's ten A.M., and our interview room in Hollywood is filled with one hundred smiling, aspiring WHEEL OF FORTUNE contestants. I welcome them and introduce our contestant coordinators. Then we get serious.

I ask, "How many of you can solve the puzzles on the show with just one or two letters showing?"

About thirty hands go up . . . some boldly . . . others on the timid side.

"Good. Then you should be able to pass the WHEEL OF FORTUNE test, because that's all we give you—one or two letters—and you have to solve fifteen puzzles in five minutes."

(Nervous laughter fills the room.)

"No one gets on WHEEL OF FORTUNE—not even Ollie North—unless he or she can pass the test."

Nancy goes on, "That's the way the WHEEL OF FORTUNE contestant interview process begins. Passing this difficult test is just the first step.

"From over six hundred applicants per week we can select only thirty to appear on the show. Ability to solve puzzles is of prime importance, but we also look for the friendly, outgoing personality, a competitive game player, and a good shopper.

"In addition to interviewing contestants in Hollywood, we travel throughout the United States auditioning people. New York, Miami, Cleveland, Atlanta, Dallas, Boston, Philadelphia, Detroit, Chicago, and Baltimore are just some of the cities we've visited. When we travel to a city, we interview one thousand people in three days! We also have lots of reporters and local television crews covering these auditions.

"Our staff of thirty works to audition and interview contestants, arranges for the prizes, and creates and researches the puzzles. Finally everything comes together in the studio on Tape Day.

"Eighty people on the studio crew have been working feverishly for twenty-four hours to get everything set. The art director and property master have the prizes beautifully displayed in showcases, the production director has worked with the camera operator, the audio engineers, and the lighting technicians to make certain everything is just right.

"It's time for the first show. The associate director begins the countdown: 'Five—four—three—two—one—tape is rolling.'

"Now we all wait—the staff, the crew, the audience, the contestants. We wait for that magic moment when someone solves the puzzle and wins the prize he or she has been dreaming about for years—the new car, the fur coat, the fabulous diamond bracelet, or a real honeymoon trip for the couple who missed out when they were first married.

"Happiness fills the studio! The applause and cheering are real! We all laugh. We all smile. We share in each contestant's triumph and joy.

"That's what it's like. And that's why it's so much fun to be the producer on WHEEL OF FORTUNE."

If you're ready to take the plunge, you can write for WHEEL OF FORTUNE contestant information at the following address:

> WHEEL OF FORTUNE Contestants
> c/o Merv Griffin Enterprises
> 1541 North Vine Street
> Hollywood, CA 90028

And remember—one lucky winner of the The Official WHEEL OF FORTUNE Puzzle Book Sweepstakes will win a trip to Hollywood to audition for the show! It could be you! Look for the special "Bonus Round" puzzle on the last page, and enter today!

GOOD LUCK!

LEVEL II

CATEGORY: THING

PUZZLE NUMBER: 51

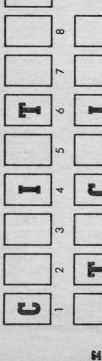

POINTS: 100 for no letters added.
Subtract 5 points for each consonant guessed.
Subtract 10 points for each vowel guessed.

TOTAL: _____

USED LETTER BOARD: ___ ___ ___ ___ ___

64

CATEGORY: **LANDMARK**

PUZZLE NUMBER: **52**

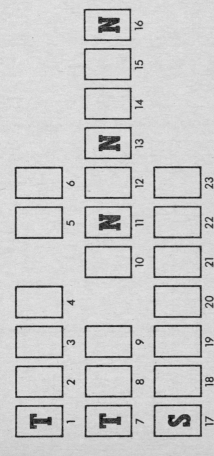

T										
1	2	3	4		5	6				

T					N		N			N
7	8	9		10	11	12	13	14	15	16

S						
17	18	19	20	21	22	23

POINTS: 100 for no letters added.
Subtract 5 points for each consonant guessed.
Subtract 10 points for each vowel guessed.

TOTAL: ________

USED LETTER BOARD: ___ ___ ___ ___ ___ ___ ___ ___

TOTAL: _____

CATEGORY: PHRASE

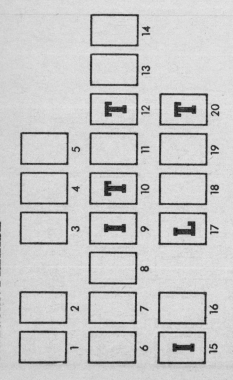

1	2	3	4	5	

| | | | T (9) | I (10) | 11 | T (12) | 13 | 14 |

POINTS: 100 for no letters added.
Subtract 5 points for each consonant guessed.
Subtract 10 points for each vowel guessed.

USED LETTER BOARD: _____

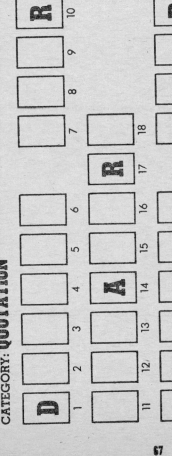

D						R
1	2	3	4	5	6	7 8 9 10

POINTS: 100 for no letters added.
Subtract 5 points for each consonant guessed.
Subtract 10 points for each vowel guessed.

USED LETTER BOARD: — — — — — — — — —

TOTAL: _____

CATEGORY: PERSON

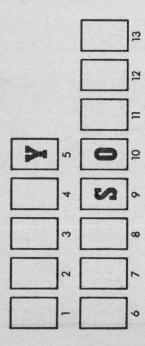

1	2	3	4	5
				Y

6	7	8	9	10	11	12	13
			S	**O**			

POINTS: 100 for no letters added.
Subtract 5 points for each consonant guessed.
Subtract 10 points for each vowel guessed.

USED LETTER BOARD:

TOTAL: _____

68

CATEGORY: **PHRASE**

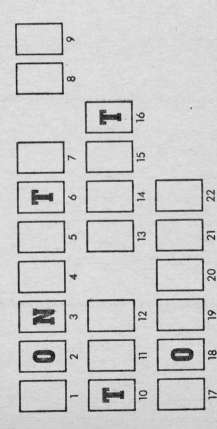

TOTAL: _____

POINTS: 100 for no letters added.
Subtract 5 points for each consonant guessed.
Subtract 10 points for each vowel guessed.

USED LETTER BOARD: — — — — — — —

69

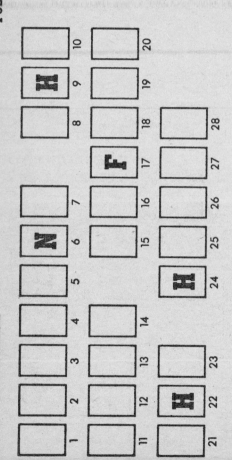

| | | | | | | **N** | | **H** | |
|1|2|3|4|5|6|7|8|9|10|

| | | | | | | | **F** | | |
|11|12|13|14|15|16|17|18|19|20|

| | | | | **H** | | | | |
|21|22|23|24|25|26|27|28|

POINTS: 100 for no letters added.
   Subtract 5 points for each consonant guessed.
   Subtract 10 points for each vowel guessed.

TOTAL: _____

USED LETTER BOARD: _____

CATEGORY: **THING**

PUZZLE NUMBER: **58**

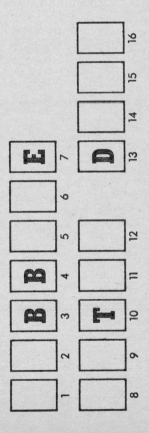

		B	B			E
1	2	3	4	5	6	7

		T				D
8	9	10	11	12	13	14	15	16

POINTS: 100 for no letters added.
Subtract 5 points for each consonant guessed.
Subtract 10 points for each vowel guessed.

TOTAL: _____

USED LETTER BOARD: — — — — — —

71

PUZZLE NUMBER: 59

CATEGORY: PERSON

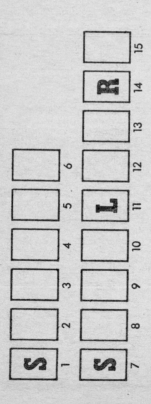

S						
1	2	3	4	5	6	

S				L			R	
7	8	9	10	11	12	13	14	15

POINTS: 100 for no letters added.
Subtract 5 points for each consonant guessed.
Subtract 10 points for each vowel guessed.

TOTAL: _____

USED LETTER BOARD: — — — — — — — — — —

72

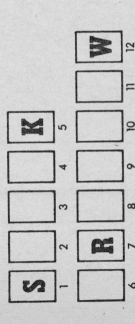

S				K
1	2	3	4	5

	R				W
6	7	8	9	10	11	12

POINTS: 100 for no letters added.
Subtract 5 points for each consonant guessed.
Subtract 10 points for each vowel guessed.

TOTAL: _____

USED LETTER BOARD: — — — — — —

73

CATEGORY: **PERSON**

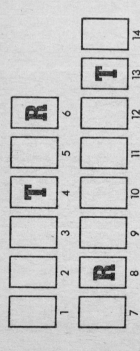

| | R | | T | | R |
|1|2|3|4|5|6|

| R | | | | | | T | |
|7|8|9|10|11|12|13|14|

POINTS: 100 for no letters added.
Subtract 5 points for each consonant guessed.
Subtract 10 points for each vowel guessed.

TOTAL: _____

USED LETTER BOARD: — — — — — — —

74

CATEGORY: **TITLE**

PUZZLE NUMBER: **62**

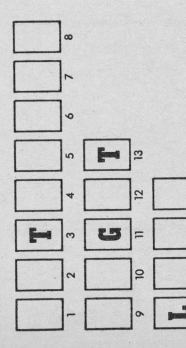

| 1 | 2 | **T** 3 | 4 | 5 | 6 | 7 | 8 |

| 9 | 10 | **G** 11 | 12 | **T** 13 |

| **L** 14 | 15 | 16 | 17 |

POINTS: 100 for no letters added.
Subtract 5 points for each consonant guessed.
Subtract 10 points for each vowel guessed.

USED LETTER BOARD: ___ ___ ___ ___

TOTAL: _____

75

CATEGORY: **PLACE**

PUZZLE NUMBER: **63**

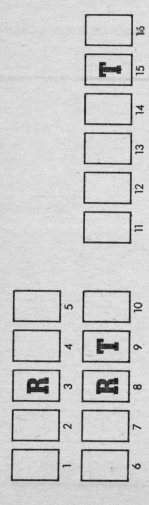

1 | 2 | **R** 3 | 4 | 5

6 | 7 | **R** 8 | **T** 9 | 10

11 | 12 | 13 | 14 | **T** 15 | 16

POINTS: 100 for no letters added.
Subtract 5 points for each consonant guessed.
Subtract 10 points for each vowel guessed.

TOTAL: _____

USED LETTER BOARD: ___ ___ ___

76

CATEGORY: **PLACE**

PUZZLE NUMBER: **64**

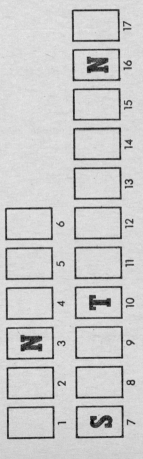

		N			
1	2	3	4	5	6

S			T		
7	8	9	10	11	12

			N	
13	14	15	16	17

POINTS: 100 for no letters added.
Subtract 5 points for each consonant guessed.
Subtract 10 points for each vowel guessed.

TOTAL: _____

USED LETTER BOARD: ___ ___ ___ ___ ___

77

CATEGORY: **PEOPLE**

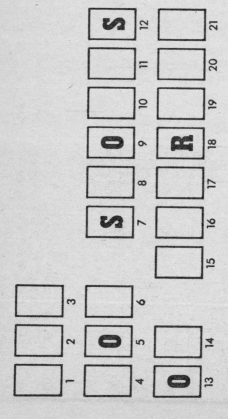

1	2	3

	O	
4	5	6

S		**O**			**S**
7	8	9	10	11	12

O		
13	14	15

	R		
16	17	18	19

20	21

POINTS: 100 for no letters added.
Subtract 5 points for each consonant guessed.
Subtract 10 points for each vowel guessed.

USED LETTER BOARD: ⎯ ⎯ ⎯ ⎯

TOTAL: ⎯⎯⎯⎯⎯

78

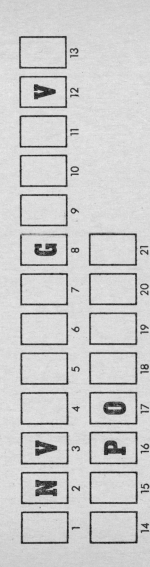

CATEGORY: **OCCUPATION**

PUZZLE NUMBER: **66**

N	V				G
2	3	4	5	6	7	8	9	10	11	12	13

(1) N (2) V (3) _ (4) _ (5) _ (6) _ (7) G (8) _ (9) _ (10) _ (11) V (12) _ (13)

P O
14 15 16 17 18 19 20 21

POINTS: 100 for no letters added.
Subtract 5 points for each consonant guessed.
Subtract 10 points for each vowel guessed.

TOTAL: _____

USED LETTER BOARD: ___ ___ ___ ___

79

CATEGORY: THINGS

PUZZLE NUMBER: 67

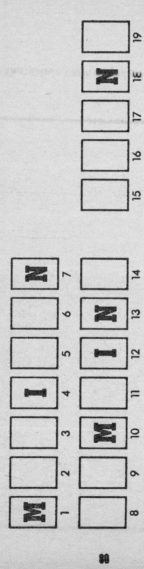

M			I			N
1	2	3	4	5	6	7

		M		I	N	
8	9	10	11	12	13	14

			N	
15	16	17	18	19

POINTS: 100 for no letters added.
Subtract 5 points for each consonant guessed.
Subtract 10 points for each vowel guessed.

TOTAL: _____

USED LETTER BOARD.

88

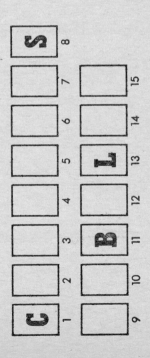

C							S
1	2	3	4	5	6	7	8

		B		L		
9	10	11	12	13	14	15

TOTAL: _____

POINTS: 100 for no letters added.
Subtract 5 points for each consonant guessed.
Subtract 10 points for each vowel guessed.

USED LETTER BOARD: __ __ __ __ __ __ __

CATEGORY: **OCCUPATION**

PUZZLE NUMBER: **69**

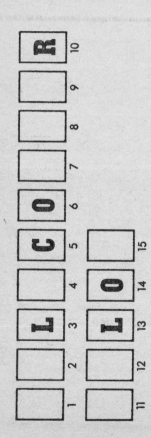

| 1 | 2 | L
3 | 4 | C
5 | O
6 | 7 | 8 | 9 | R
10 |

| 11 | 12 | L
13 | O
14 | 15 |

POINTS: 100 for no letters added.
Subtract 5 points for each consonant guessed.
Subtract 10 points for each vowel guessed.

TOTAL: _____

USED LETTER BOARD: ___ ___ ___ ___

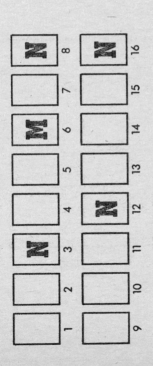

| 1 | 2 | N 3 | 4 | 5 | M 6 | 7 | N 8 |
| 9 | 10 | 11 | 12 | 13 | 14 | 15 | N 16 |

TOTAL: _____

POINTS: 100 for no letters added.
Subtract 5 points for each consonant guessed.
Subtract 10 points for each vowel guessed.

USED LETTER BOARD: — — — —

CATEGORY: THING

PUZZLE NUMBER: 71

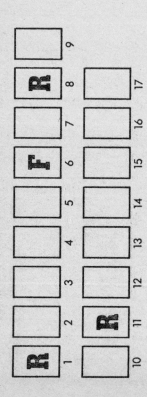

R					F		R	
1	2	3	4	5	6	7	8	9

	R						
10	11	12	13	14	15	16	17

POINTS: 100 for no letters added.
Subtract 5 points for each consonant guessed.
Subtract 10 points for each vowel guessed.

TOTAL: _____

USED LETTER BOARD:

84

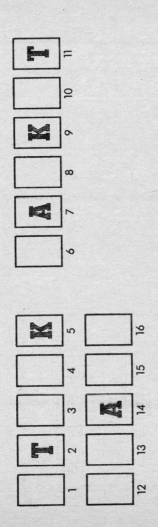

TOTAL: _____

POINTS: 100 for no letters added.
Subtract 5 points for each consonant guessed.
Subtract 10 points for each vowel guessed.

USED LETTER BOARD: _ _ _ _ _ _ _

CATEGORY: **THING**

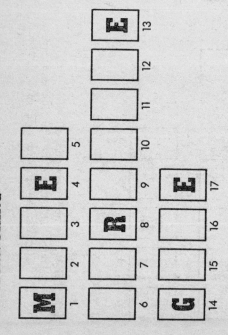

M			E	
1	2	3	4	5

			R	E	
6	7	8	9	10	11	12	13

G			E	
14	15	16	17

POINTS: 100 for no letters added.
Subtract 5 points for each consonant guessed.
Subtract 10 points for each vowel guessed.

TOTAL: _____

USED LETTER BOARD: _ _ _ _

86

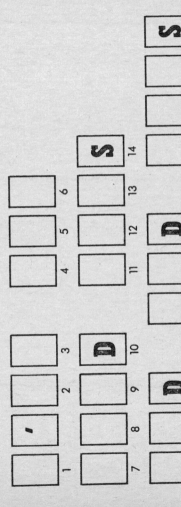

POINTS: 100 for no letters added.
Subtract 5 points for each consonant guessed.
Subtract 10 points for each vowel guessed.

TOTAL: _____

USED LETTER BOARD: — — — — — — —

87

CATEGORY: **OCCUPATION**

PUZZLE NUMBER: **75**

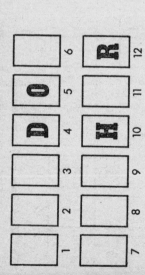

1	2	3	**D** 4	**O** 5	6
7	8	9	**H** 10	11	**R** 12

POINTS: 100 for no letters added.
Subtract 5 points for each consonant guessed.
Subtract 10 points for each vowel guessed.

TOTAL: _____

USED LETTER BOARD: _ _ _ _ _

CATEGORY: **PHRASE**

PUZZLE NUMBER: **76**

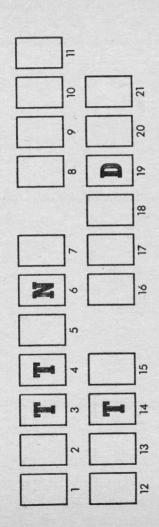

| 1 | 2 | **T** 3 | **T** 4 | 5 | **N** 6 | 7 | | 8 | 9 | 10 | 11 |

| 12 | 13 | **T** 14 | 15 | | 16 | 17 | 18 | **D** 19 | 20 | 21 |

POINTS: 100 for no letters added.
Subtract 5 points for each consonant guessed.
Subtract 10 points for each vowel guessed.

TOTAL: _____

USED LETTER BOARD: ___ ___ ___ ___ ___

CATEGORY: **PEOPLE**

TOTAL: _____

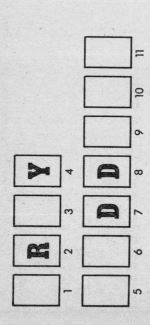

	R		Y
1	2	3	4

		D	D
5	6	7	8

9	10	11

POINTS: 100 for no letters added.
   Subtract 5 points for each consonant guessed.
   Subtract 10 points for each vowel guessed.

USED LETTER BOARD: _ _ _ _ _ _ _

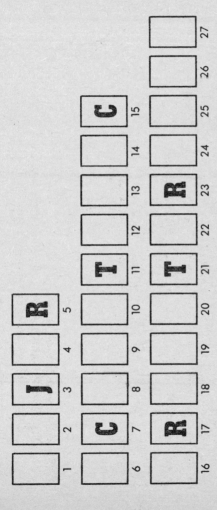

1	2	J 3	4	R 5

| C
7 | | | | |

6	C 7	8	9	10	T 11	12	13	14	C 15

R 16	R 17	18	19	20	T 21	22	R 23	24	25	26	27

POINTS: 100 for no letters added.
Subtract 5 points for each consonant guessed.
Subtract 10 points for each vowel guessed.

TOTAL: _____

USED LETTER BOARD: ___ ___ ___ ___

91

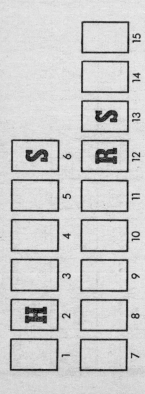

1	H 2	3	4	5	S 6

7	8	9	10	11	R 12	S 13	14	15

TOTAL: _____

POINTS: 100 for no letters added.
Subtract 5 points for each consonant guessed.
Subtract 10 points for each vowel guessed.

USED LETTER BOARD: __ __ __ __ __

CATEGORY: **THINGS** PUZZLE NUMBER: **80**

		T		M			S
1	2	3	4	5	6	7	8

9	10	11

M			E				S
12	13	14	15	16	17	18	19

POINTS: 100 for no letters added.
Subtract 5 points for each consonant guessed.
Subtract 10 points for each vowel guessed.

TOTAL: ________

USED LETTER BOARD: ___ ___ ___ ___ ___ ___ ___ ___

CATEGORY: **PHRASE**

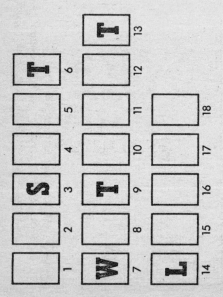

		S			T
1	2	3	4	5	6

W		T				T
7	8	9	10	11	12	13

L				
14	15	16	17	18

POINTS: 100 for no letters added.
Subtract 5 points for each consonant guessed.
Subtract 10 points for each vowel guessed.

TOTAL: _____

USED LETTER BOARD: _____ _____ _____

94

CATEGORY: **PHRASE**

PUZZLE NUMBER: **82**

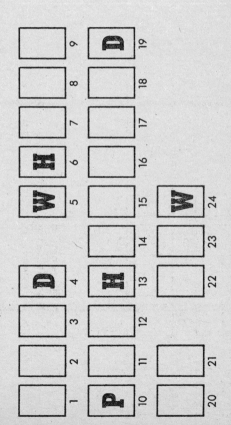

			D	W	H			
1	2	3	4	5	6	7	8	9

P			H					D
10	11	12	13	14	15	16	17	18	19

				W
20	21	22	23	24

POINTS: 100 for no letters added.
Subtract 5 points for each consonant guessed.
Subtract 10 points for each vowel guessed.

USED LETTER BOARD: ___ ___ ___ ___

TOTAL: _____

95

CATEGORY: **FICTIONAL CHARACTER**

PUZZLE NUMBER: **83**

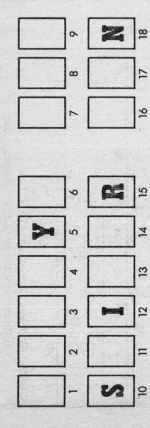

1	2	3	4	Y (5)	6		7	8	9
S (10)	11	I (12)	13	14	R (15)		16	17	N (18)

POINTS: 100 for no letters added.
Subtract 5 points for each consonant guessed.
Subtract 10 points for each vowel guessed.

TOTAL: _____

USED LETTER BOARD: — — — — — —

96

CATEGORY: **TITLE**

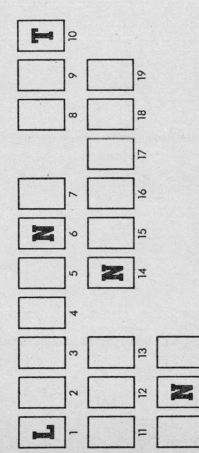

L					N				T
1	2	3	4	5	6	7	8	9	10

		N					
11	12	13	14	15	16	17	18	19

	N	
20	21	22

POINTS: 100 for no letters added.
      Subtract 5 points for each consonant guessed.
      Subtract 10 points for each vowel guessed.

USED LETTER BOARD: _____

TOTAL: _____

97

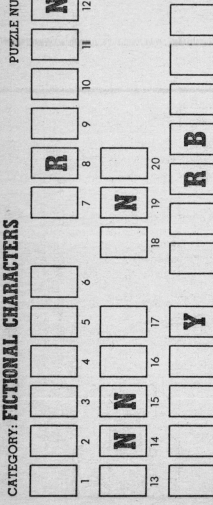

CATEGORY: FICTIONAL CHARACTERS

PUZZLE NUMBER: 85

1 | 2 | 3 | 4 | 5 | 6 | 7 | **R** (8) | 9 | 10 | **N** (11) | **N** (12)

13 | **N** (14) | **N** (15) | 16 | 17 | 18 | **N** (19) | 20

21 | 22 | 23 | 24 | **Y** (25) | 26 | 27 | **R** (28) | **B** (29) | 30 | 31 | 32 | 33

POINTS: 100 for no letters added.
Subtract 5 points for each consonant guessed.
Subtract 10 points for each vowel guessed.

USED LETTER BOARD: — — — — — — TOTAL: _____

98

CATEGORY: **PERSON**

PUZZLE NUMBER: **86**

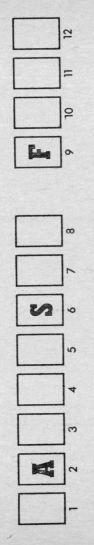

	A				S				F			
1	2	3	4	5	6	7	8	9	10	11	12

POINTS: 100 for no letters added.
Subtract 5 points for each consonant guessed.
Subtract 10 points for each vowel guessed.

TOTAL: _____

USED LETTER BOARD: ___ ___ ___

99

CATEGORY: **PHRASE**

PUZZLE NUMBER: **87**

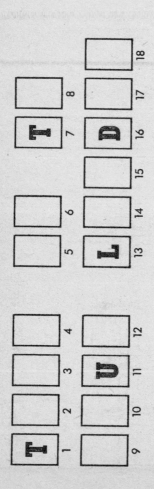

| T | | | |
| 1 | 2 | 3 | 4 |

| | | | T | |
| 5 | 6 | 7 | 8 |

| | | | U | |
| 9 | 10 | 11 | 12 |

| L | | | D |
| 13 | 14 | 15 | 16 |

| | |
| 17 | 18 |

POINTS: 100 for no letters added.
Subtract 5 points for each consonant guessed.
Subtract 10 points for each vowel guessed.

TOTAL: _____

USED LETTER BOARD: ___ ___ ___ ___ ___

100

CATEGORY: PHRASE

PUZZLE NUMBER: 88

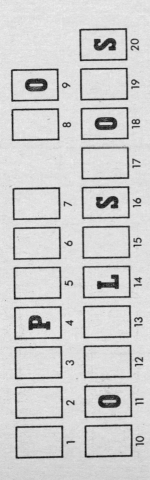

1	2	3	P (4)	5	6	7	(8)	O (9)

| O (10) | O (11) | 12 | 13 | L (14) | 15 | S (16) | 17 | O (18) | 19 | S (20) |

POINTS: 100 for no letters added.
Subtract 5 points for each consonant guessed.
Subtract 10 points for each vowel guessed.

TOTAL: _____

USED LETTER BOARD: — — — — — — —

101

CATEGORY: **PERSON**

PUZZLE NUMBER: **89**

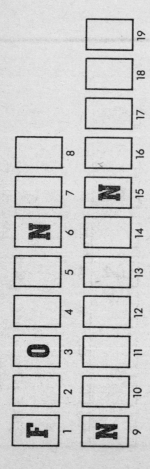

F		O			N		
1	2	3	4	5	6	7	8

N					N				
9	10	11	12	13	14	15	16	17	18	19

POINTS: 100 for no letters added.
        Subtract 5 points for each consonant guessed.
        Subtract 10 points for each vowel guessed.

TOTAL: _____

USED LETTER BOARD: _ _ _ _

102

CATEGORY: PERSON

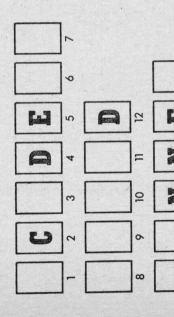

	C		D	E		
1	2	3	4	5	6	7

				D	
8	9	10	11	12	

		N	N	E	
13	14	15	16	17	18

POINTS: 100 for no letters added.
Subtract 5 points for each consonant guessed.
Subtract 10 points for each vowel guessed.

TOTAL: _____

USED LETTER BOARD: ___ ___ ___ ___

103

CATEGORY: **QUOTATION**

PUZZLE NUMBER: **91**

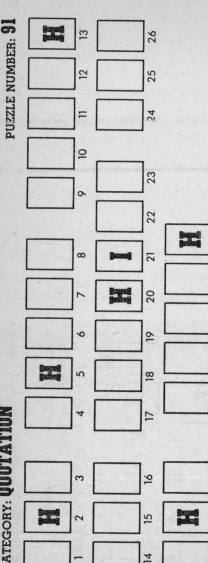

POINTS: 100 for no letters added.
Subtract 5 points for each consonant guessed.
Subtract 10 points for each vowel guessed.

USED LETTER BOARD: _____

TOTAL: _____

104

CATEGORY: **THING**

PUZZLE NUMBER: **92**

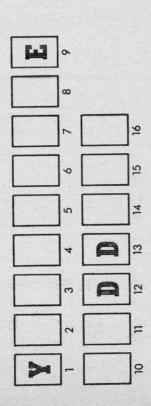

POINTS: 100 for no letters added.
Subtract 5 points for each consonant guessed.
Subtract 10 points for each vowel guessed.

TOTAL: _____

USED LETTER BOARD: ___ | ___ | ___ | ___

CATEGORY: **TITLE**

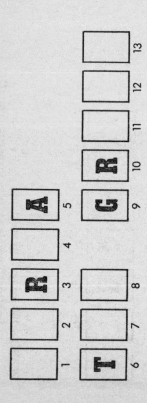

		R		A
1	2	3	4	5

T			G	R
6	7	8	9	10

11	12	13

POINTS: 100 for no letters added.
Subtract 5 points for each consonant guessed.
Subtract 10 points for each vowel guessed.

TOTAL: _____

USED LETTER BOARD: ___ ___ ___

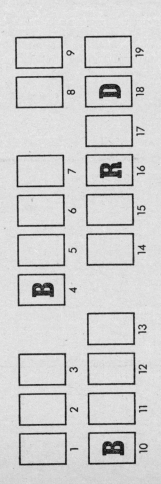

| | | | | | B | | | | 9 |
|1|2|3|4|5|6|7|8| |

| B | | | | | | R | | D | 19 |
|10|11|12|13|14|15|16|17|18| |

POINTS: 100 for no letters added.
 Subtract 5 points for each consonant guessed.
 Subtract 10 points for each vowel guessed.

TOTAL: _____

USED LETTER BOARD: ____ ____ ____ ____

107

CATEGORY: OCCUPATION

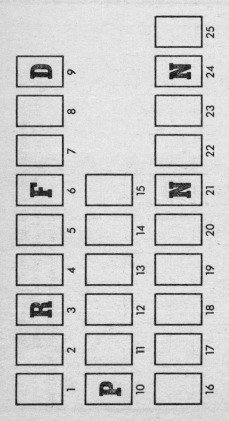

		R			F			D
1	2	3	4	5	6	7	8	9

P					
10	11	12	13	14	15

					N			N	
16	17	18	19	20	21	22	23	24	25

POINTS: 100 for no letters added.
Subtract 5 points for each consonant guessed.
Subtract 10 points for each vowel guessed.

TOTAL: _____

USED LETTER BOARD: — — — —

108

CATEGORY: PERSON

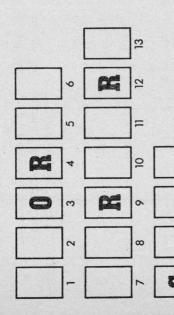

TOTAL: _____

POINTS: 100 for no letters added.
Subtract 5 points for each consonant guessed.
Subtract 10 points for each vowel guessed.

USED LETTER BOARD: ___ ___ ___ ___ ___

CATEGORY: QUOTATION

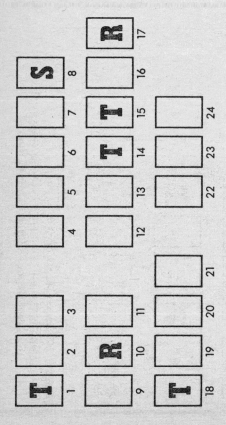

T							S
1	2	3	4	5	6	7	8

	R				T	T	R
9	10	11	12	13	14	15	16	17

T						
18	19	20	21	22	23	24

POINTS: 100 for no letters added.
   Subtract 5 points for each consonant guessed.
   Subtract 10 points for each vowel guessed.

TOTAL: _____

USED LETTER BOARD: ___ ___ ___ ___

110

CATEGORY: **PERSON**

PUZZLE NUMBER: **98**

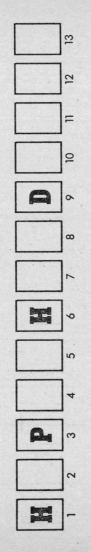

H		P			H			D				
1	2	3	4	5	6	7	8	9	10	11	12	13

POINTS: 100 for no letters added.
Subtract 5 points for each consonant guessed.
Subtract 10 points for each vowel guessed.

TOTAL: _____

USED LETTER BOARD: ___ ___ ___ ___

111

CATEGORY: QUOTATION

PUZZLE NUMBER: 99

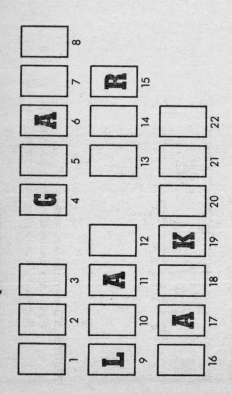

POINTS: 100 for no letters added.
Subtract 5 points for each consonant guessed.
Subtract 10 points for each vowel guessed.

TOTAL: _____

USED LETTER BOARD: — — — —

112

CATEGORY: **THING**

PUZZLE NUMBER: **100**

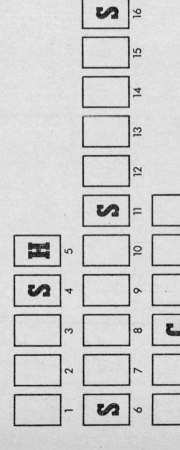

1	2	3	**S** 4	**H** 5

S 6	7	8	9	10	**S** 11

12	13	14	15	**S** 16

17	18	**C** 19	20	21	22

TOTAL: _____

POINTS: 100 for no letters added.
Subtract 5 points for each consonant guessed.
Subtract 10 points for each vowel guessed.

USED LETTER BOARD: ___ ___ ___ ___

113

WHEEL OF
FORTUNE "TRIVIA" (as of 8/1/87)

Number of Shows Taped to Date:
over 4,000

Number of Contestants Who Have Appeared on Show:
12,172

Number of Cars Given Away:
1,012

Total Prize Money Since Inception of Show:
Over one billion dollars

Most Won by One Contestant:
$64,461 by Judy Bongarzone of Los Angeles

Oldest Contestant:
92 years old

Youngest Contestant:
13 years old

Foreign Contestants:
There have been British and Canadian citizens who have appeared on WHEEL.

Number of Times Puzzles Guessed From One Letter:
Three. One such puzzle was "I Before E Except After C," which was solved with only the letter *t* exposed.

Number of Viewers Daily:
42 million, including daytime and nighttime versions

Number of Stations That Carry the Show:
208 nighttime, 205 daytime

Most Times Show Appears in One Market in a Day:
There are many markets where the show appears four or five times a day, including network, syndicated, and cable stations.

Fan Mail:
3,000 pieces of fan mail come in during any given week.

Vanna's Dresses:
Vanna wears 450 different dresses per year and repeats some of them.

Most Expensive Prize:
A $60,000 log cabin

Keep the Tape Rolling:
On taping days, WHEEL does five shows and has taped as many as sixty in one month

Studio Audience:
250 fans watch the tapings in the studio.

Wheel and Hope:
WHEEL OF FORTUNE is taped in Burbank at NBC Studio Four. It's the same studio where Bob Hope tapes his specials.

Puzzles:
The show chews up forty-five puzzles per week.

Born to Shop:
WHEEL's producer, Nancy Jones, takes one day per week to do nothing but shop for the prizes given away on the show.

Your Host and Hostess:
Chuck Woolery was the original host of WHEEL OF FORTUNE. He is now hosting *Love Connection.* Susan Stafford was the original hostess. She left the show to pursue a career outside of show business.

Dimensions:
The puzzle board is thirteen feet high, and the wheel is seven feet eight inches.

More Dimensions:
Vanna is five feet six inches. She wears a size 4 dress.

Money Matters:
The largest sum of money on the wheel during the nighttime version is five thousand dollars. Daytime's largest sum is two thousand dollars.

Wheel Music:
The music you hear on WHEEL OF FORTUNE was composed by Merv Griffin. He also composed the theme for *Jeopardy*—another game show he created.

More Money Matters:
In 1986, Merv Griffin sold his company to The Coca-Cola Company and in doing so, sold WHEEL OF FORTUNE with it. How valuable are game shows? Coke paid Merv more than 200 million dollars.

You Want It, You Got It:
WHEEL OF FORTUNE is already booked through 1992 on some stations.

Most Inexpensive Prize:
20-dollar pack of playing cards

Most Money Lost to Bankrupt:
11,000 dollars

Prize Chosen Most Often:
Ceramic dalmatian

Prize Never Chosen:
Home wine-cellar

Wheel of Fortune Staff:
It takes twenty-five people to bring you WHEEL OF FORTUNE every day, not including camera and technical crew.

Producer:
Nancy Jones, WHEEL's producer, has been in charge of the show for thirteen years.

Winners and Sex:
There are more women contestants than men, therefore more female winners.

It Ain't That Easy:
Sixty-five percent of the people who try the WHEEL written exam fail.

Bringing the WHEEL Home:
You can buy WHEEL OF FORTUNE board games, computer software, watches, shirts, electronic games, with more licensees being added monthly.

Vanna's Secret:
Vanna knows the answers to the puzzles prior to the show's taping. But she knows how to keep a secret.

All in the Family:
WHEEL OF FORTUNE is directed by former *Merv Griffin Show* director, Dick Carson. Dick's brother, Johnny Carson, is also in the television business.

WHEEL Worldwide:
WHEEL OF FORTUNE'S format is licensed in several foreign countries, including France, where the French "WHEEL" is number one in its time slot.

LEVEL III

CATEGORY: **PLACE**

PUZZLE NUMBER: **101**

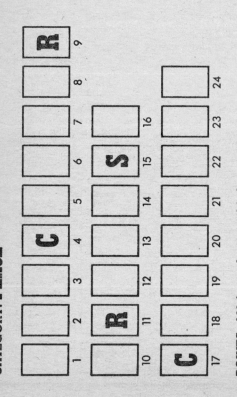

			C					R
1	2	3	4	5	6	7	8	9

C	R				S		
10	11	12	13	14	15	16	

C							
17	18	19	20	21	22	23	24

POINTS: 100 for no letters added.
Subtract 5 points for each consonant guessed.
Subtract 10 points for each vowel guessed.

TOTAL: _____

USED LETTER BOARD: __ __ __ __ __ __ __ __

120

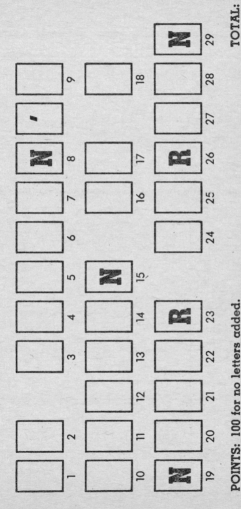

| | | | | | | | N | ' | |
|1|2|3|4|5|6|7|8|9|

POINTS: 100 for no letters added.
Subtract 5 points for each consonant guessed.
Subtract 10 points for each vowel guessed.

TOTAL: _____

USED LETTER BOARD: ___ ___ ___ ___

121

CATEGORY: **PHRASE**

PUZZLE NUMBER: 103

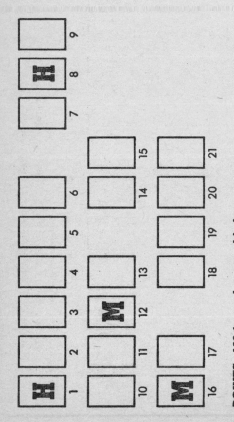

H							**H**	
1	2	3	4	5	6	7	8	9

		M				
10	11	12	13	14	15	

M					
16	17	18	19	20	21

POINTS: 100 for no letters added.
Subtract 5 points for each consonant guessed.
Subtract 10 points for each vowel guessed.

TOTAL: _____

USED LETTER BOARD: ___ ___ ___ ___

122

CATEGORY: **PHRASE**

PUZZLE NUMBER: 104

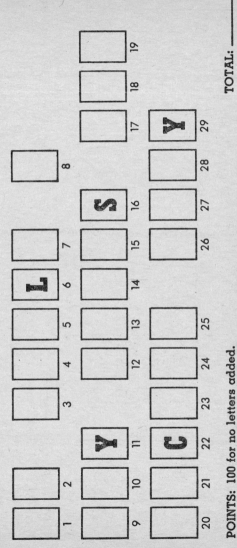

| 1 | 2 | 3 | 4 | 5 | 6 L | 7 | 8 |

| 9 | 10 | 11 Y | 12 | 13 | 14 | 15 | 16 S | 17 | 18 | 19 |

| 20 | 21 | 22 C | 23 | 24 | 25 | 26 | 27 | 28 | 29 Y |

POINTS: 100 for no letters added.
Subtract 5 points for each consonant guessed.
Subtract 10 points for each vowel guessed.

TOTAL: _____

USED LETTER BOARD: ___ ___ ___ ___

123

PUZZLE NUMBER: 105

CATEGORY: PLACE

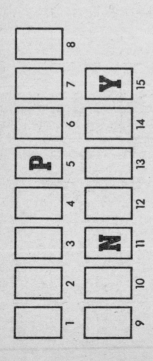

1	2	3	4	5	6	7	8
				P			

9	10	11	12	13	14	15
		N				Y

POINTS: 100 for no letters added.
Subtract 5 points for each consonant guessed.
Subtract 10 points for each vowel guessed.

TOTAL: _____

USED LETTER BOARD: — — — — — — — —

CATEGORY: TITLE

PUZZLE NUMBER: 106

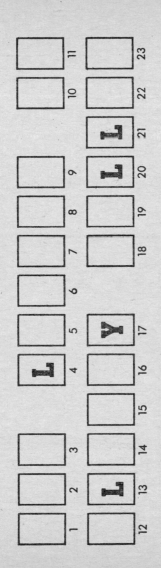

POINTS: 100 for no letters added.
Subtract 5 points for each consonant guessed.
Subtract 10 points for each vowel guessed.

USED LETTER BOARD: — — — — — — —

TOTAL: _____

125

CATEGORY: THING

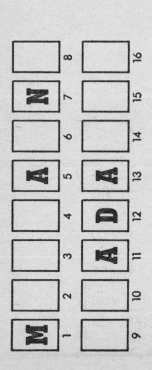

M				A		N	
1	2	3	4	5	6	7	8

		A	D	A			
9	10	11	12	13	14	15	16

POINTS: 100 for no letters added.
Subtract 5 points for each consonant guessed.
Subtract 10 points for each vowel guessed.

TOTAL: _____

USED LETTER BOARD: — — — — — —

CATEGORY: **PLACE**

PUZZLE NUMBER: **108**

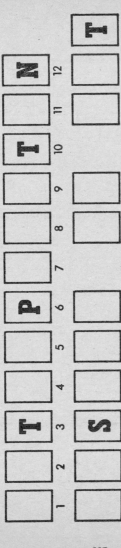

| | | T | | | P | | | | T | | N |
|1|2|3|4|5|6|7|8|9|10|11|12|

| S | | | | | | | | T |
|13|14|15|16|17|18|19|20|21|22|23|

POINTS: 100 for no letters added.
Subtract 5 points for each consonant guessed.
Subtract 10 points for each vowel guessed.

TOTAL: _____

USED LETTER BOARD: — — — — — — —

127

CATEGORY: **EVENT**

PUZZLE NUMBER: **109**

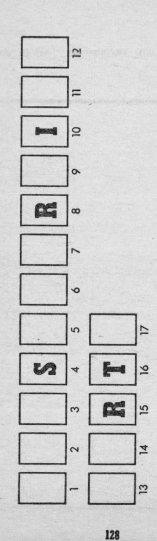

			S				R		I		
1	2	3	4	5	6	7	8	9	10	11	12

	R	T	
13	14 15	16	17

POINTS: 100 for no letters added.
Subtract 5 points for each consonant guessed.
Subtract 10 points for each vowel guessed.

TOTAL: _____

USED LETTER BOARD: ___ ___ ___ ___

128

CATEGORY: **FICTIONAL CHARACTER**　　PUZZLE NUMBER: **110**

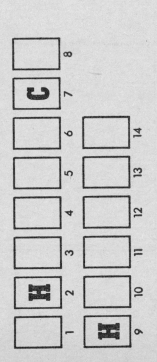

| | H | | | | | C | |
|1|2|3|4|5|6|7|8|

| H | | | | | |
|9|10|11|12|13|14|

POINTS: 100 for no letters added.
Subtract 5 points for each consonant guessed.
Subtract 10 points for each vowel guessed.

TOTAL: _____

USED LETTER BOARD: _ _ _ _ _ _ _

129

CATEGORY: **THING**

PUZZLE NUMBER: **111**

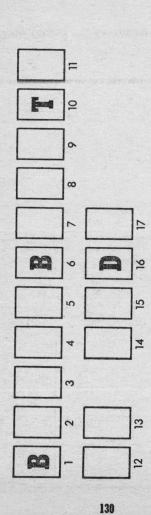

B 1 2 3 4 5 **B** 6 7 8 9 **T** 10 11

12 13 14 15 **D** 16 17

POINTS: 100 for no letters added.
Subtract 5 points for each consonant guessed.
Subtract 10 points for each vowel guessed.

TOTAL: _____

USED LETTER BOARD: ___ ___ ___

130

CATEGORY: **QUOTATION** PUZZLE NUMBER: **112**

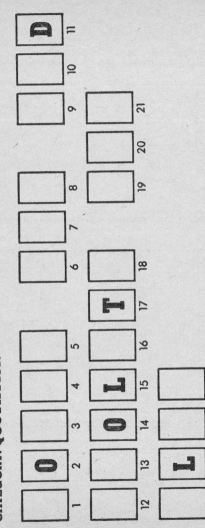

1	2	3	4	5		6	7	8		9	10	11
	O											D

12	13	14	15	16	17	18		19	20	21
		O	L		T					

22	23	24	25
	L		

POINTS: 100 for no letters added.
Subtract 5 points for each consonant guessed.
Subtract 10 points for each vowel guessed.

TOTAL: ________

USED LETTER BOARD: ___ ___ ___ ___ ___ ___ ___ ___

CATEGORY: **PLACE**

PUZZLE NUMBER: **113**

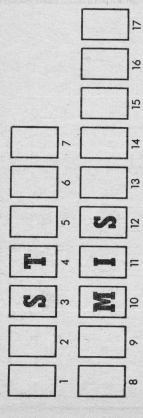

1 2 3 **S** 4 **T** 5 6 7

8 9 10 **M** 11 **I** 12 **S** 13 14 15 16 17

POINTS: 100 for no letters added.
Subtract 5 points for each consonant guessed.
Subtract 10 points for each vowel guessed.

USED LETTER BOARD: _____ _____ _____

TOTAL: _____

PUZZLE NUMBER: 114

CATEGORY: PLACE

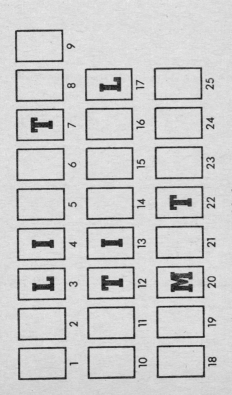

| 1 | 2 | L 3 | I 4 | 5 | 6 | T 7 | 8 | 9 |

| 10 | 11 | T 12 | I 13 | 14 | 15 | 16 | L 17 |

| 18 | 19 | M 20 | 21 | T 22 | 23 | 24 | 25 |

POINTS: 100 for no letters added.
Subtract 5 points for each consonant guessed.
Subtract 10 points for each vowel guessed.

TOTAL: _____

USED LETTER BOARD: ___ ___ ___ ___

133

CATEGORY: **PERSON**

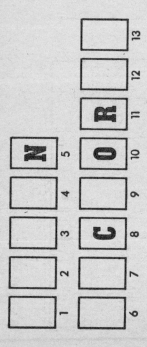

				N
1	2	3	4	5

			O	R
6	7	C	9	10	11

TOTAL: _____

POINTS: 100 for no letters added.
Subtract 5 points for each consonant guessed.
Subtract 10 points for each vowel guessed.

USED LETTER BOARD: _____ _____ _____

134

CATEGORY: **PHRASE**

PUZZLE NUMBER: 116

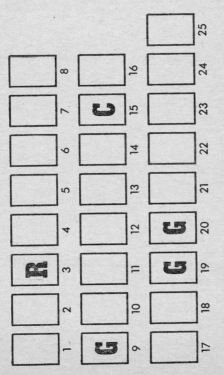

| | | **R** | | | | | |
|1|2|3|4|5|6|7|8|

| **G** | | | | | | **C** | |
|9|10|11|12|13|14|15|16|

| | | **G** | **G** | | | | |
|17|18|19|20|21|22|23|24|25|

POINTS: 100 for no letters added.
  Subtract 5 points for each consonant guessed.
  Subtract 10 points for each vowel guessed.

USED LETTER BOARD: _____ | _____ | _____

TOTAL: _____

135

CATEGORY: **EVENT**

PUZZLE NUMBER: **117**

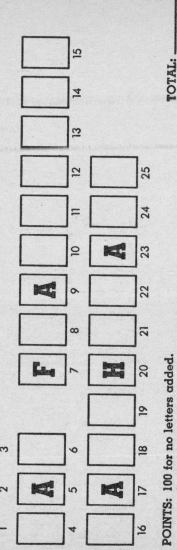

| | H | | | | A | | F | | | | | | | |
|1|2|3| |4|5|6|7|8|9|10|11|12|13|14|15|

| A | | | H | | A | | | | | |
|16|17|18|19|20|21|22|23|24|25|

POINTS: 100 for no letters added.
Subtract 5 points for each consonant guessed.
Subtract 10 points for each vowel guessed.

TOTAL: _____

USED LETTER BOARD: ____ ____ ____ ____

136

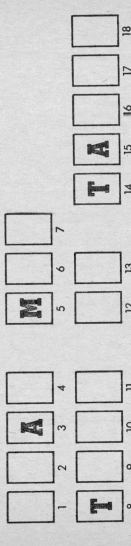

		A		M		
1	2	3	4	5	6	7

T			
8	9	10	11

		T	A			
12	13	14	15	16	17	18

TOTAL: _____

POINTS: 100 for no letters added.
Subtract 5 points for each consonant guessed.
Subtract 10 points for each vowel guessed.

USED LETTER BOARD: — — — — — — — —

137

CATEGORY: **THINGS**

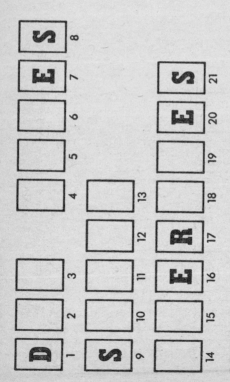

D						E	S
1	2	3	4	5	6	7	8

S				
9	10	11	12	13

	E	R	E	S
14	16	17	20	21

POINTS: 100 for no letters added.
　　　　Subtract 5 points for each consonant guessed.
　　　　Subtract 10 points for each vowel guessed.

TOTAL: _____

USED LETTER BOARD: _____ _____ _____

138

CATEGORY: PLACE

PUZZLE NUMBER: 120

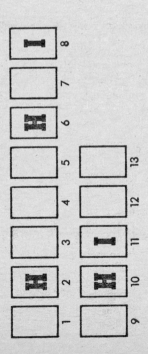

H			H		I
1	2	3	4	5	6	7	8

POINTS: 100 for no letters added.
Subtract 5 points for each consonant guessed.
Subtract 10 points for each vowel guessed.

TOTAL: _____

USED LETTER BOARD: — — — — —

139

CATEGORY: **TITLE**

PUZZLE NUMBER: **121**

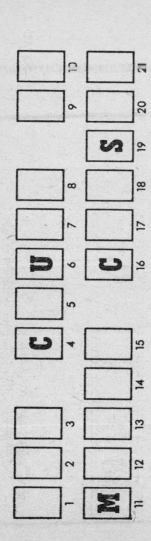

| | | | C | | U | | | 9 | CI |
|1|2|3|4|5|6|7|8| | |

| M | | | | | C | | S | | |
|11|13|14|15|16| |19|20|21| |

POINTS: 100 for no letters added.
Subtract 5 points for each consonant guessed.
Subtract 10 points for each vowel guessed.

TOTAL: _____

USED LETTER BOARD: —— —— —— —— —— ——

140

TOTAL: _____

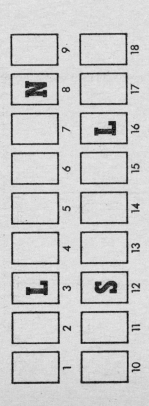

POINTS: 100 for no letters added.
Subtract 5 points for each consonant guessed.
Subtract 10 points for each vowel guessed.

USED LETTER BOARD: _____

141

CATEGORY: **QUOTATION**

PUZZLE NUMBER: **123**

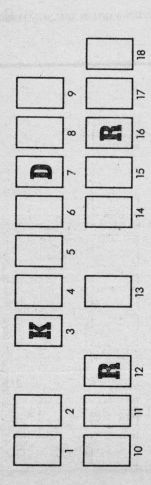

		K				D		
1	2	3	4	5	6	7	8	9

	R						R	
10	11	12	13	14	15	16	17	18

POINTS: 100 for no letters added.
Subtract 5 points for each consonant guessed.
Subtract 10 points for each vowel guessed.

TOTAL: _____

USED LETTER BOARD: ___ ___ ___ ___ ___

142

CATEGORY: **PHRASE**

PUZZLE NUMBER: 124

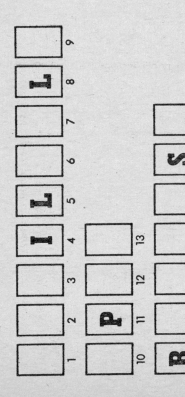

| 1 | 2 | 3 | **I**4 | **L**5 | 6 | 7 | **L**8 | 9 |

| **R**14 | **P**11 |

POINTS: 100 for no letters added.
Subtract 5 points for each consonant guessed.
Subtract 10 points for each vowel guessed.

TOTAL: _____

USED LETTER BOARD: _____ _____

143

CATEGORY: **EVENT**

PUZZLE NUMBER: **125**

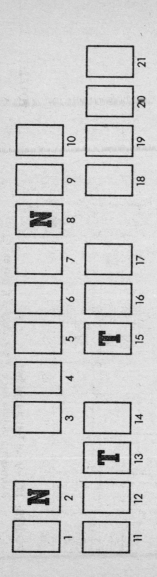

1	N 2	3	4	5	6	7	N 8	9	10

11	12	T 13	14	T 15	16	17	18	19	20	21

POINTS: 100 for no letters added.
Subtract 5 points for each consonant guessed.
Subtract 10 points for each vowel guessed.

TOTAL: _____

USED LETTER BOARD: _____ _____ _____

144

CATEGORY: **PHRASE**

PUZZLE NUMBER: **126**

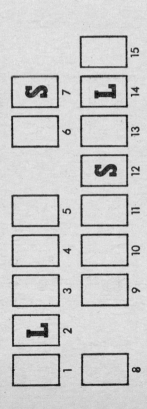

| | L | | | | | S | |
|1|2|3|4|5|6|7| |

| | | | | S | | L | |
|8|9|10|11|12|13|14|15|

POINTS: 100 for no letters added.
Subtract 5 points for each consonant guessed.
Subtract 10 points for each vowel guessed.

USED LETTER BOARD: —————————

TOTAL: ————

145

CATEGORY: PLACE

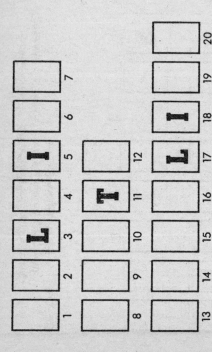

PUZZLE NUMBER: 127

		L		**I**		
1	2	3	4	5	6	7

			T		
8	9	10	11	12

				L	**I**		
13	14	15	16	17	18	19	20

POINTS: 100 for no letters added.
Subtract 5 points for each consonant guessed.
Subtract 10 points for each vowel guessed.

TOTAL: _____

USED LETTER BOARD: ___ ___ ___

146

CATEGORY: **PLACE**

PUZZLE NUMBER: **128**

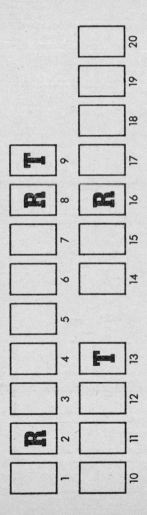

	R						R	T
1	2	3	4	5	6	7	8	9

			T			R		
10	11	12	13	14	15	16	17	18	19	20

POINTS: 100 for no letters added.
Subtract 5 points for each consonant guessed.
Subtract 10 points for each vowel guessed.

TOTAL: _____

USED LETTER BOARD: ___ ___ ___ ___ ___ ___

147

CATEGORY: PHRASE

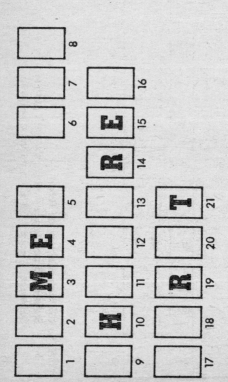

| 1 | 2 | 3 M | 4 E | 5 | 6 | 7 | 8 |

| 9 | 10 H | 11 | 12 | 13 | 14 R | 15 E | 16 |

| 17 | 18 | 19 R | 20 | 21 T |

POINTS: 100 for no letters added.
Subtract 5 points for each consonant guessed.
Subtract 10 points for each vowel guessed.

USED LETTER BOARD: ___ ___ ___

TOTAL: ___

148

CATEGORY: **PERSON**

PUZZLE NUMBER: **130**

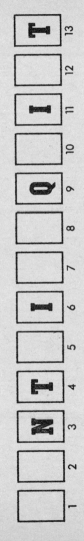

		N	T		I			Q		I		T
1	2	3	4	5	6	7	8	9	10	11	12	13

POINTS: 100 for no letters added.
Subtract 5 points for each consonant guessed.
Subtract 10 points for each vowel guessed.

TOTAL: _____

USED LETTER BOARD: _____ _____ _____ _____

149

CATEGORY: **PERSON**

PUZZLE NUMBER: 131

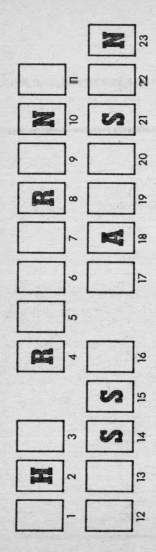

	H		R				R		N		
1	2	3	4	5	6	7	8	9	10	11	
		S	S								
			14	15								

(grid with letters: position 2 = H, 4 = R, 8 = R, 10 = N, 14 = S, 15 = S, 18 = A, 21 = S, 22 = I, 23 = N)

POINTS: 100 for no letters added.
    Subtract 5 points for each consonant guessed.
    Subtract 10 points for each vowel guessed.

TOTAL: _____

USED LETTER BOARD: _____

150

CATEGORY: **QUOTATION**

PUZZLE NUMBER: **132**

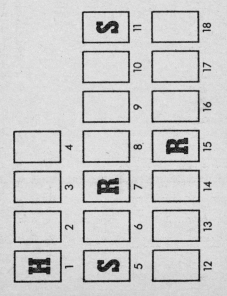

H			
1	2	3	4

S		R	S
5	6	7	8	9	10	11

		R	
12	13	14	15	16	17	18

POINTS: 100 for no letters added.
    Subtract 5 points for each consonant guessed.
    Subtract 10 points for each vowel guessed.

TOTAL: _____

USED LETTER BOARD: ___ ___ ___ ___ ___ ___

CATEGORY: **PEOPLE**

PUZZLE NUMBER: **133**

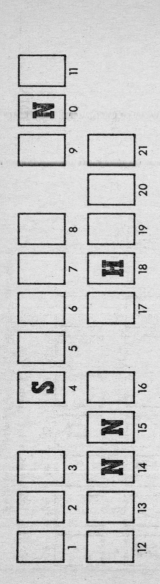

| 1 | 2 | 3 | | S (4) | 5 | 6 | 7 | 8 | | 9 | N (0) | 11 |

Row 2: 12 | 13 | N (14) | N (15) | 16 | 17 | H (18) | 19 | 20 | 21

POINTS: 100 for no letters added.
Subtract 5 points for each consonant guessed.
Subtract 10 points for each vowel guessed.

TOTAL: _____

USED LETTER BOARD: _____

152

CATEGORY: OCCUPATION

PUZZLE NUMBER: 134

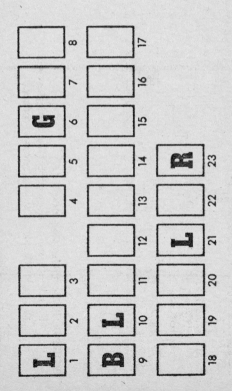

L					G		
1	2	3	4	5	6	7	8

B	L						
9	10	11	12	13	14	15	16	17

				L		R
18	19	20	21	22	23

POINTS: 100 for no letters added.
Subtract 5 points for each consonant guessed.
Subtract 10 points for each vowel guessed.

TOTAL: _____

USED LETTER BOARD: —— —— —— —— —— ——

152

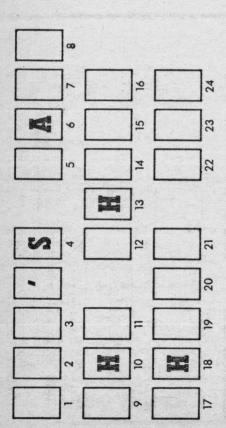

CATEGORY: PHRASE

PUZZLE NUMBER: 135

1	2	3		S 4	-	A 6	7	8

H 10

H 13

| 9 | 10 | 11 | 12 | 13 | 14 | 15 | 16 |

| 17 | 18 | 19 | 20 | 21 | 22 | 23 | 24 |

POINTS: 100 for no letters added.
Subtract 5 points for each consonant guessed.
Subtract 10 points for each vowel guessed.

TOTAL: _____

USED LETTER BOARD: _____

154

CATEGORY: **PLACE**

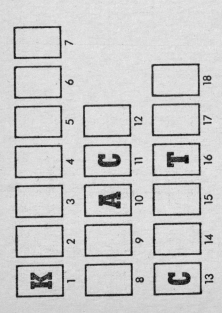

K						
1	2	3	4	5	6	7

		A	C		
8	9	10	11	12	

C			T		
13	14	15	16	17	18

POINTS: 100 for no letters added.
Subtract 5 points for each consonant guessed.
Subtract 10 points for each vowel guessed.

USED LETTER BOARD: —— —— ——

TOTAL: ————

155

CATEGORY: **PHRASE**

PUZZLE NUMBER: **137**

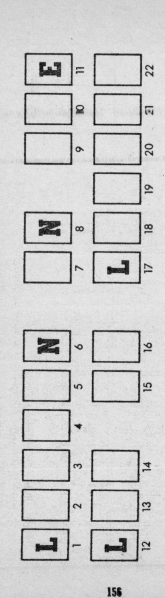

L				N	
1	2	3	4	5	6

	N				E
7	8	9	10	11	

L					
12	13	14	15	16	

	L				
17	18	19	20	21	22

POINTS: 100 for no letters added.
    Subtract 5 points for each consonant guessed.
    Subtract 10 points for each vowel guessed.

TOTAL: _____

USED LETTER BOARD: _____

156

CATEGORY: QUOTATION

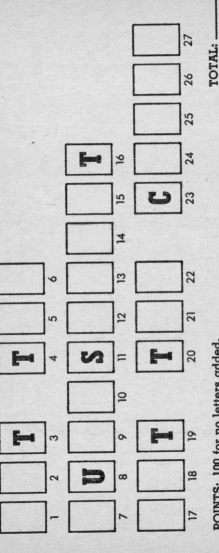

| | | T | | | |
|1|2| T (3) | T (4) |5| 6 |

Row 2: U (8), S (11), T (16)

Row 3: T (19), T (20), C (23), T (16)

POINTS: 100 for no letters added.
Subtract 5 points for each consonant guessed.
Subtract 10 points for each vowel guessed.

TOTAL: _____

USED LETTER BOARD: — — — — — — —

157

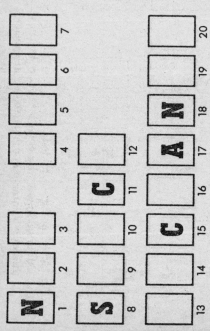

CATEGORY: **PLACE**

PUZZLE NUMBER: **139**

N						
1	2	3	4	5	6	7

S			C		
8	9	10	11	12	

		C		A	N
13	14	15	16	17	18

19	20

TOTAL: _____

POINTS: 100 for no letters added.
Subtract 5 points for each consonant guessed.
Subtract 10 points for each vowel guessed.

USED LETTER BOARD:

158

CATEGORY: PHRASE

PUZZLE NUMBER: 140

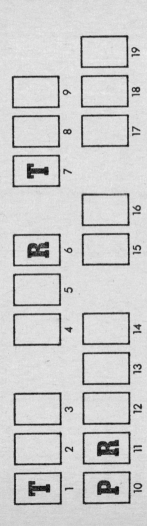

T					R	T		
1	2	3	4	5	6	7	8	9

P	R							
10	11	12	13	14	15	16	17	18	19

POINTS: 100 for no letters added.
Subtract 5 points for each consonant guessed.
Subtract 10 points for each vowel guessed.

USED LETTER BOARD: —————— ———

TOTAL: ———————

159

CATEGORY: **TITLE**

TOTAL: _____

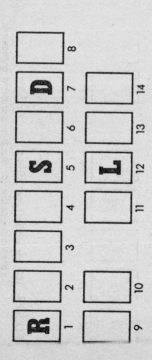

| R | | | | S | | D | |
| 1 | 2 | 3 | 4 | 5 | 6 | 7 | 8 |

| | | L | | |
| 9 | 10 | 11 | 12 | 13 | 14 |

POINTS: 100 for no letters added.
Subtract 5 points for each consonant guessed.
Subtract 10 points for each vowel guessed.

USED LETTER BOARD: _____

CATEGORY: **PLACE**

PUZZLE NUMBER: **142**

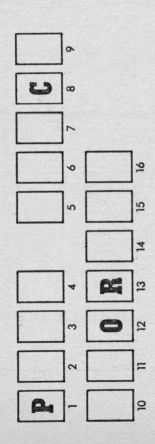

P							C	
1	2	3	4	5	6	7	8	9

	O	R			
10	11	12	13	14	15	16

POINTS: 100 for no letters added.
Subtract 5 points for each consonant guessed.
Subtract 10 points for each vowel guessed.

TOTAL: _____

USED LETTER BOARD: ___ ___ ___ ___ ___ ___ ___

161

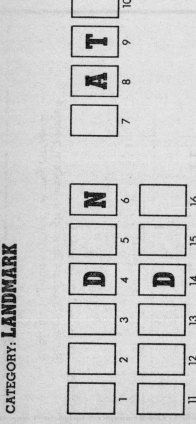

			D		N			A	T	
1	2	3	4	5	6	7	8	9	10	

			D		
11	12	13	14	15	16

POINTS: 100 for no letters added.
　　　　Subtract 5 points for each consonant guessed.
　　　　Subtract 10 points for each vowel guessed.

TOTAL: _____

USED LETTER BOARD: ___ ___ ___ ___ ___

162

CATEGORY: **THING**

PUZZLE NUMBER: **144**

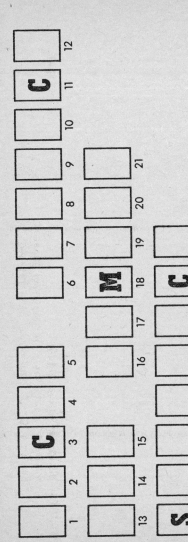

| | | **C** | | **5** | | | | **9** | **10** | **C** | |
|1|2|3|4| |6|7|8| | |11|12|

POINTS: 100 for no letters added.
Subtract 5 points for each consonant guessed.
Subtract 10 points for each vowel guessed.

TOTAL: _____

USED LETTER BOARD: — — — — — — — —

163

CATEGORY: PLACE

PUZZLE NUMBER: 145

1	2	3	4	5	6
		L	L		

7	8	9	10	
	O	R		

TOTAL: _____

POINTS: 100 for no letters added.
Subtract 5 points for each consonant guessed.
Subtract 10 points for each vowel guessed.

USED LETTER BOARD: _____ _____ _____

164

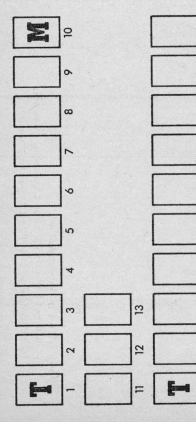

T									M
1	2	3	4	5	6	7	8	9	10

11	12	13

T									
14	15	16	17	18	19	20	21	22	23

POINTS: 100 for no letters added.
    Subtract 5 points for each consonant guessed.
    Subtract 10 points for each vowel guessed.

USED LETTER BOARD: ⎯ ⎯ ⎯ ⎯ ⎯

TOTAL: ⎯⎯⎯⎯

165

CATEGORY: **FICTIONAL CHARACTER**

PUZZLE NUMBER: 147

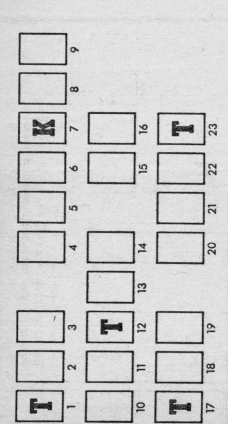

POINTS: 100 for no letters added.
Subtract 5 points for each consonant guessed.
Subtract 10 points for each vowel guessed.

TOTAL: _____

USED LETTER BOARD: _____ _____ _____

166

CATEGORY: **EVENT**

PUZZLE NUMBER: **148**

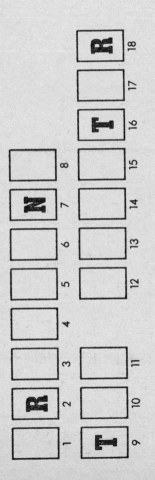

	R					N	
1	2	3	4	5	6	7	8

T						T		R
9	10	11	12	13	14	15	16	17	18

POINTS: 100 for no letters added.
Subtract 5 points for each consonant guessed.
Subtract 10 points for each vowel guessed.

TOTAL: _____

USED LETTER BOARD: — — — — — — — —

167

CATEGORY: PERSON

PUZZLE NUMBER: 149

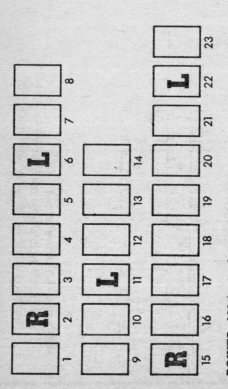

1	R 2	3	4	5	L 6	7	8

9	10	L 11	12	13	14

R 15	16	17	18	19	20	21	L 22	23

POINTS: 100 for no letters added.
Subtract 5 points for each consonant guessed.
Subtract 10 points for each vowel guessed.

TOTAL: _____

USED LETTER BOARD: — — — — — —

168

CATEGORY: **PLACE**

PUZZLE NUMBER: **150**

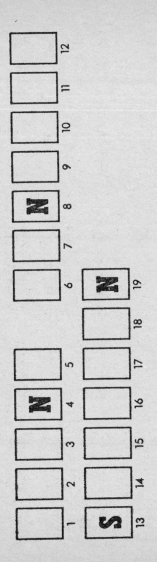

| 1 | 2 | 3 | 4 (N) | 5 | 6 | 7 | 8 (N) | 9 | 10 | 11 | 12 |

| 13 (S) | 14 | 15 | 16 | 17 | 18 | 19 (N) |

POINTS: 100 for no letters added.
Subtract 5 points for each consonant guessed.
Subtract 10 points for each vowel guessed.

TOTAL: _____

USED LETTER BOARD: — — — — — —

A

1. 1
2. 19, 26
3. 0
4. 8
5. 3, 7, 13
6. 6, 10
7. 3
8. 1, 8
9. 10, 14
10. 1, 4
11. 8, 12
12. 2, 5
13. 5, 11
14. 2
15. 7
16. 0
17. 0
18. 0
19. 2
20. 4
21. 2
22. 3, 12
23. 0
24. 4, 7
25. 0
26. 6, 10, 17
27. 4, 14
28. 15, 18
29. 2, 9, 13
30. 5, 13
31. 2, 8, 13
32. 8, 16
33. 13
34. 4, 12
35. 0
36. 1, 15
37. 6, 10
38. 11
39. 0
40. 0

41. 8
42. 1, 3, 7, 11, 18
43. 5
44. 0
45. 9, 12
46. 12, 25
47. 10, 19, 22
48. 5, 24
49. 9, 13
50. 11
51. 8
52. 0
53. 11
54. 14
55. 2, 8
56. 0
57. 12
58. 2, 5, 9
59. 0
60. 4
61. 2
62. 2, 7
63. 2, 12, 16
64. 6, 15
65. 15, 21
66. 9
67. 6, 17
68. 0
69. 0
70. 5, 11
71. 0
72. 7, 14
73. 6, 11
74. 15, 19
75. 8
76. 8, 10
77. 1
78. 2, 19

79. 5
80. 4, 9, 17
81. 1, 16
82. 23
83. 11, 17
84. 0
85. 11, 13, 18, 22, 27
86. 2
87. 2, 15
88. 0
89. 17
90. 1, 3, 8, 10
91. 14
92. 0
93. 5
94. 0
95. 16, 23
96. 11, 16
97. 6, 9, 20
98. 12
99. 6, 11, 17
100. 13
101. 2, 24
102. 11, 18
103. 2
104. 1, 3, 8, 10, 26, 28
105. 4, 13
106. 0
107. 5, 11, 13
108. 11, 21
109. 7, 14
110. 0
111. 4, 9
112. 6, 19
113. 0
114. 1, 11, 16
115. 13

116. 2, 7, 13
117. 5, 8, 17, 23
118. 3, 15
119. 14, 18
120. 3, 7, 13
121. 0
122. 10, 15, 18
123. 13
124. 1, 3, 6
125. 1, 3
126. 4, 6, 8
127. 2, 14, 20
128. 3, 18
129. 6
130. 0
131. 18
132. 17
133. 2, 5, 7, 9, 13, 16
134. 2, 7, 11, 15, 20
135. 6
136. 10
137. 13
138. 0
139. 17
140. 0
141. 3
142. 2, 7, 16
143. 8
144. 2, 13, 19, 23
145. 2
146. 11
147. 0
148. 15
149. 3, 12
150. 3, 11, 15

B

1. 0	39. 0	77. 5	114. 0
2. 0	40. 0	78. 16	115. 0
3. 0	41. 0	79. 0	116. 0
4. 0	42. 0	80. 0	117. 0
5. 0	43. 12	81. 2	118. 0
6. 0	44. 0	82. 15, 20	119. 0
7. 1	45. 0	83. 0	120. 0
8. 0	46. 7	84. 17	121. 0
9. 4	47. 16	85. 29	122. 4
10. 0	48. 7, 14	86. 0	123. 0
11. 1	49. 0	87. 0	124. 7
12. 13	50. 0	88. 0	125. 0
13. 0	51. 0	89. 0	126. 0
14. 10	52. 4	90. 0	127. 0
15. 0	53. 0	91. 24	128. 0
16. 0	54. 4, 22	92. 0	129. 0
17. 0	55. 0	93. 4	130. 0
18. 0	56. 13	94. 4, 10	131. 0
19. 0	57. 15	95. 12	132. 0
20. 0	58. 3, 4	96. 7	133. 0
21. 0	59. 12	97. 12	134. 9
22. 14	60. 0	98. 0	135. 0
23. 0	61. 0	99. 0	136. 0
24. 0	62. 0	100. 0	137. 0
25. 0	63. 0	101. 10, 22	138. 0
26. 16	64. 0	102. 0	139. 0
27. 0	65. 4	103. 0	140. 0
28. 0	66. 0	104. 0	141. 11
29. 0	67. 15	105. 1	142. 5
30. 0	68. 11	106. 0	143. 11
31. 0	69. 0	107. 0	144. 1
32. 0	70. 1	108. 0	145. 0
33. 0	71. 0	109. 0	146. 0
34. 0	72. 0	110. 0	147. 0
35. 0	73. 0	111. 1, 6	148. 0
36. 7	74. 18	112. 22	149. 0
37. 0	75. 0	113. 0	150. 0
38. 0	76. 0		

C

1. 0
2. 0
3. 0
4. 0
5. 0
6. 0
7. 4
8. 0
9. 0
10. 8, 9
11. 0
12. 0
13. 0
14. 0
15. 9
16. 1, 7
17. 1
18. 19
19. 16
20. 0
21. 1
22. 0
23. 0
24. 0
25. 0
26. 0
27. 0
28. 0
29. 15
30. 4
31. 0
32. 3, 11, 13
33. 5, 12
34. 0
35. 6, 10
36. 13, 18
37. 11
38. 6, 8

39. 0
40. 0
41. 1
42. 0
43. 0
44. 3
45. 10
46. 20
47. 0
48. 4
49. 0
50. 7
51. 1, 13
52. 0
53. 0
54. 0
55. 0
56. 21
57. 11
58. 1, 11
59. 0
60. 0
61. 7
62. 0
63. 0
64. 0
65. 8, 20
66. 0
67. 5
68. 1
69. 5
70. 0
71. 0
72. 4, 12
73. 0
74. 0
75. 0
76. 0

77. 0
78. 7, 15
79. 0
80. 0
81. 0
82. 0
83. 0
84. 0
85. 31
86. 0
87. 0
88. 10, 13
89. 7
90. 2
91. 0
92. 0
93. 0
94. 0
95. 1, 15, 17, 18
96. 0
97. 0
98. 5, 13
99. 0
100. 19
101. 4, 17
102. 3, 21
103. 0
104. 22
105. 0
106. 0
107. 14
108. 0
109. 0
110. 7
111. 3
112. 0
113. 0

114. 18
115. 8
116. 15
117. 11, 14
118. 0
119. 12
120. 9
121. 4, 16
122. 0
123. 0
124. 0
125. 9
126. 1
127. 13
128. 0
129. 9
130. 0
131. 19
132. 0
133. 0
134. 12, 16
135. 5
136. 11, 13
137. 0
138. 23
139. 11, 15
140. 13
141. 0
142. 8
143. 0
144. 3, 11, 28
145. 0
146. 0
147. 6, 13
148. 1
149. 0
150. 6

D

1. 7
2. 3, 8, 18, 21, 29
3. 4, 10
4. 1, 7, 11
5. 14
6. 0
7. 8, 14
8. 6
9. 9
10. 0
11. 5, 10, 11, 17
12. 0
13. 13
14. 7, 13
15. 0
16. 0
17. 9
18. 4
19. 0
20. 11
21. 0
22. 0
23. 0
24. 0
25. 4
26. 15
27. 13
28. 19
29. 12
30. 3
31. 10, 15, 17
32. 9
33. 0
34. 0
35. 0
36. 0
37. 0

38. 0
39. 0
40. 0
41. 4, 7
42. 12
43. 9
44. 0
45. 0
46. 14
47. 12, 20
48. 20
49. 6, 12, 15, 16, 24
50. 13
51. 0
52. 20
53. 0
54. 1, 19
55. 0
56. 0
57. 0
58. 13
59. 0
60. 0
61. 0
62. 6
63. 11
64. 17
65. 0
66. 0
67. 0
68. 0
69. 0
70. 0
71. 10
72. 0
73. 3
74. 10, 17, 20
75. 4

76. 19
77. 7, 8
78. 0
79. 0
80. 11
81. 0
82. 4, 19
83. 0
84. 0
85. 20, 21, 23, 24
86. 12
87. 16
88. 0
89. 0
90. 4, 12
91. 16
92. 12, 13
93. 0
94. 18
95. 9
96. 13
97. 7
98. 9
99. 22
100. 0
101. 0
102. 7
103. 0
104. 9, 20
105. 3
106. 9
107. 12
108. 0
109. 0
110. 0
111. 16
112. 11
113. 0

114. 0
115. 0
116. 12, 25
117. 0
118. 1, 4
119. 1
120. 0
121. 0
122. 0
123. 7
124. 0
125. 5
126. 0
127. 0
128. 0
129. 8, 13
130. 0
131. 11
132. 0
133. 11
134. 18
135. 0
136. 6
137. 0
138. 0
139. 0
140. 0
141. 7
142. 15
143. 4, 14
144. 15, 25
145. 0
146. 5, 8, 13, 18, 21
147. 9
148. 0
149. 9
150. 5

E

1. 3, 5, 19
2. 4, 6, 9, 17, 24, 28
3. 8, 14
4. 12, 15, 20
5. 0
6. 13
7. 15
8. 11
9. 3, 5, 18
10. 14, 17, 20
11. 7
12. 9, 11
13. 0
14. 8, 14
15. 6, 13
16. 14, 16
17. 15
18. 12, 13, 20
19. 5, 12, 17, 23
20. 3, 10, 12
21. 0
22. 7
23. 6, 8, 11, 13
24. 6
25. 3, 14
26. 3, 14, 20
27. 6, 11
28. 9, 14, 17
29. 4, 7, 16, 21
30. 2, 8, 12, 16
31. 11, 16
32. 12, 15
33. 6, 15
34. 7, 9, 14
35. 15
36. 10, 12
37. 2, 4, 18
38. 0
39. 3
40. 3, 8, 11, 22

41. 5, 10, 15
42. 9, 13, 17, 20
43. 3, 11
44. 12
45. 6, 15
46. 8, 21
47. 4, 8
48. 8
49. 5, 8, 11, 17, 21, 23
50. 3, 5, 15
51. 0
52. 9, 22
53. 2, 7, 13
54. 6, 13, 18, 24
55. 7, 12
56. 4, 12, 14
57. 10, 16, 20, 23, 28
58. 7
59. 3, 5, 10, 13
60. 3, 8, 11
61. 5, 14
62. 17
63. 0
64. 2, 4, 12
65. 3, 17
66. 4, 13, 20
67. 2, 16
68. 3, 7, 14, 15
69. 2, 9
70. 2
71. 5, 12
72. 10
73. 4, 13, 17
74. 3, 12, 22
75. 11
76. 2, 20
77. 10
78. 9, 18

79. 8, 11
80. 15
81. 4, 15, 18
82. 7, 9, 18
83. 4, 6, 9
84. 18, 22
85. 6, 17
86. 0
87. 4, 6, 14, 17
88. 0
89. 5, 8, 19
90. 5, 17
91. 3, 8, 29
92. 9
93. 8, 11, 12
94. 3, 5
95. 2, 8
96. 2, 6, 8
97. 5, 11, 13, 16, 24
98. 0
99. 3, 10
100. 8, 9, 15, 21
101. 8
102. 14, 22, 25
103. 9, 13, 21
104. 7, 13, 14, 19
105. 6
106. 3, 5, 7, 14, 15
107. 8, 10, 16
108. 2, 16
109. 5
110. 3, 13
111. 11
112. 4, 8, 10, 16, 21, 25
113. 2, 5, 9, 15, 17
114. 19, 21, 23
115. 3, 4

116. 4, 16, 21, 24
117. 3, 16, 25
118. 2, 6, 9, 17
119. 7, 16, 20
120. 0
121. 3, 15
122. 2, 9
123. 18
124. 9, 15, 18
125. 7, 10, 16, 21
126. 3, 15
127. 4
128. 11, 15
129. 4, 15
130. 2
131. 3, 5, 7, 9, 13, 16
132. 4, 12, 14
133. 21
134. 5, 19, 22
135. 2, 11, 16
136. 2, 5, 12, 14, 17
137. 11
138. 2, 6, 14, 22, 27
139. 2, 13, 20
140. 9, 14, 19
141. 14
142. 6
143. 5, 10, 16
144. 7
145. 5, 11
146. 3, 4, 7, 16, 17, 20, 22, 23
147. 3, 8, 19, 21
148. 11, 12
149. 10, 19, 21
150. 7

F

1. 0	39. 4	77. 0	114. 0
2. 0	40. 0	78. 13	115. 0
3. 0	41. 0	79. 9, 10	116. 0
4. 0	42. 0	80. 0	117. 7
5. 0	43. 0	81. 0	118. 0
6. 0	44. 0	82. 0	119. 0
7. 0	45. 0	83. 0	120. 0
8. 0	46. 22	84. 11	121. 10
9. 0	47. 0	85. 0	122. 0
10. 0	48. 0	86. 9	123. 10
11. 0	49. 0	87. 0	124. 0
12. 0	50. 0	88. 0	125. 0
13. 0	51. 0	89. 1	126. 0
14. 0	52. 6	90. 0	127. 0
15. 1, 8	53. 0	91. 0	128. 1, 6
16. 4, 10	54. 29	92. 0	129. 17
17. 0	55. 0	93. 0	130. 0
18. 0	56. 0	94. 9	131. 0
19. 19, 22	57. 17	95. 6	132. 0
20. 7	58. 0	96. 0	133. 0
21. 0	59. 0	97. 0	134. 0
22. 10	60. 0	98. 0	135. 23, 24
23. 1	61. 0	99. 13	136. 0
24. 0	62. 0	100. 0	137. 16
25. 1, 5	63. 1	101. 0	138. 17
26. 0	64. 0	102. 0	139. 0
27. 0	65. 14	103. 15, 20	140. 4, 16
28. 0	66. 0	104. 0	141. 0
29. 17	67. 0	105. 0	142. 10
30. 0	68. 0	106. 11	143. 0
31. 0	69. 0	107. 0	144. 0
32. 0	70. 9	108. 20	145. 7
33. 3, 10	71. 6	109. 0	146. 0
34. 0	72. 0	110. 0	147. 16
35. 0	73. 0	111. 13	148. 0
36. 0	74. 0	112. 0	149. 1
37. 0	75. 0	113. 0	150. 0
38. 1	76. 0		

G

1. 4	39. 6, 11	77. 0	114. 6
2. 0	40. 20	78. 26	115. 0
3. 0	41. 0	79. 0	116. 9, 19, 20
4. 4	42. 8	80. 0	117. 0
5. 11	43. 10	81. 0	118. 0
6. 0	44. 7	82. 0	119. 19
7. 0	45. 0	83. 0	120. 5
8. 0	46. 0	84. 7	121. 0
9. 16	47. 1, 9	85. 0	122. 0
10. 0	48. 0	86. 0	123. 6
11. 13	49. 3	87. 0	124. 0
12. 0	50. 0	88. 7	125. 0
13. 4, 20	51. 17	89. 11, 16	126. 0
14. 0	52. 0	90. 0	127. 6
15. 0	53. 0	91. 23	128. 14
16. 0	54. 0	92. 16	129. 0
17. 0	55. 0	93. 9	130. 0
18. 1, 7	56. 0	94. 0	131. 0
19. 0	57. 7	95. 0	132. 10
20. 0	58. 6	96. 1, 5	133. 0
21. 0	59. 15	97. 0	134. 6
22. 8	60. 0	98. 0	135. 21
23. 0	61. 0	99. 4	136. 0
24. 11	62. 11	100. 0	137. 6
25. 0	63. 4	101. 0	138. 0
26. 12	64. 1	102. 0	139. 19
27. 0	65. 0	103. 6	140. 0
28. 0	66. 8	104. 0	141. 0
29. 0	67. 14	105. 12	142. 0
30. 0	68. 0	106. 6	143. 1, 7, 15
31. 0	69. 0	107. 3	144. 0
32. 0	70. 0	108. 0	145. 10
33. 1	71. 17	109. 12	146. 0
34. 6	72. 0	110. 0	147. 0
35. 1	73. 14	111. 0	148. 8
36. 0	74. 4, 7	112. 0	149. 0
37. 1	75. 0	113. 0	150. 1
38. 0	76. 1, 7		

H

1. 10
2. 0
3. 6
4. 5, 17
5. 0
6. 9
7. 0
8. 0
9. 2
10. 0
11. 0
12. 4, 10
13. 8, 14, 21
14. 0
15. 0
16. 0
17. 0
18. 8
19. 11
20. 9
21. 0
22. 0
23. 5
24. 18
25. 0
26. 2
27. 0
28. 6, 16
29. 6
30. 0
31. 5
32. 0
33. 0
34. 0
35. 0
36. 14
37. 0
38. 0

39. 2, 7, 16
40. 2
41. 11
42. 16
43. 2
44. 8
45. 2
46. 4
47. 0
48. 0
49. 0
50. 2
51. 2
52. 8
53. 1, 4, 6
54. 0
55. 1
56. 1, 11
57. 9, 24
58. 12
59. 0
60. 0
61. 0
62. 12
63. 10
64. 0
65. 2
66. 0
67. 0
68. 2
69. 1
70. 0
71. 0
72. 16
73. 0
74. 0
75. 10
76. 15

77. 0
78. 22, 27
79. 2
80. 0
81. 10
82. 6, 13
83. 8
84. 0
85. 10
86. 1
87. 0
88. 0
89. 12
90. 0
91. 2, 5, 13, 20, 28, 34
92. 6
93. 7
94. 2, 13
95. 0
96. 15
97. 4, 19
98. 1, 6
99. 0
100. 5
101. 16
102. 10
103. 1, 8
104. 18
105. 9
106. 2, 18
107. 9, 15
108. 0
109. 1
110. 2, 9
111. 0
112. 0
113. 8, 14

114. 0
115. 0
116. 0
117. 2, 20
118. 0
119. 0
120. 2, 6, 10
121. 2
122. 0
123. 14
124. 0
125. 14, 16
126. 10
127. 7, 12
128. 0
129. 10
130. 0
131. 2
132. 1
133. 18
134. 0
135. 10, 13, 18
136. 0
137. 10
138. 5, 12, 21
139. 16
140. 8
141. 2
142. 9
143. 0
144. 29
145. 0
146. 0
147. 2, 14, 18
148. 10
149. 0
150. 0

I

1. 8, 11, 17
2. 1
3. 2, 7, 12
4. 3, 10, 13
5. 9
6. 2, 5
7. 7, 13
8. 0
9. 13
10. 7, 10
11. 6
12. 7
13. 2, 15, 19
14. 3, 12
15. 0
16. 6, 11
17. 0
18. 6, 17
19. 4, 8, 15, 21
20. 14
21. 8
22. 0
23. 16
24. 0
25. 7
26. 0
27. 9
28. 3, 7
29. 0
30. 0
31. 0
32. 10
33. 2, 9, 11
34. 0
35. 2, 14
36. 8, 17
37. 13, 15

38. 4, 12
39. 5, 9, 12, 14
40. 12, 15, 18
41. 0
42. 6, 14
43. 8
44. 5
45. 3, 13
46. 2, 6, 19
47. 2
48. 0
49. 2, 19
50. 0
51. 4, 15
52. 21
53. 9, 15
54. 0
55. 0
56. 8, 20
57. 5
58. 0
59. 9
60. 10
61. 12
62. 10, 15
63. 0
64. 9
65. 19
66. 1, 7, 11
67. 4, 12
68. 6, 12
69. 4, 12
70. 7, 15
71. 15
72. 0
73. 7
74. 1

75. 2
76. 5, 13
77. 9
78. 8, 12, 14
79. 0
80. 2, 6, 13
81. 8
82. 3, 14, 16
83. 12
84. 5
85. 2, 16
86. 5
87. 0
88. 5, 17
89. 10, 14
90. 14
91. 21
92. 7, 14
93. 0
94. 0
95. 5, 7, 14
96. 0
97. 0
98. 11
99. 5, 20
100. 1, 3, 18
101. 12, 14, 23
102. 1, 20
103. 4, 11, 19
104. 0
105. 0
106. 0
107. 2, 6
108. 9
109. 10
110. 0
111. 2
112. 13

113. 11
114. 4, 13
115. 7, 12
116. 11
117. 12
118. 0
119. 0
120. 8, 11
121. 18
122. 17
123. 4
124. 4
125. 6, 12
126. 11
127. 5, 18
128. 0
129. 11, 18
130. 6, 8, 11
131. 0
132. 8
133. 19
134. 0
135. 19
136. 0
137. 2, 4, 7
138. 10, 18, 25
139. 0
140. 12
141. 9
142. 14
143. 13
144. 27
145. 0
146. 0
147. 5, 11
148. 6
149. 7
150. 17

J

1. 0	39. 0	77. 0	114. 0
2. 0	40. 0	78. 3	115. 0
3. 0	41. 0	79. 7	116. 0
4. 0	42. 0	80. 0	117. 0
5. 0	43. 0	81. 0	118. 0
6. 0	44. 0	82. 0	119. 4
7. 0	45. 0	83. 0	120. 0
8. 0	46. 15	84. 0	121. 0
9. 0	47. 0	85. 0	122. 0
10. 16	48. 0	86. 0	123. 0
11. 0	49. 0	87. 0	124. 0
12. 0	50. 0	88. 1	125. 0
13. 0	51. 0	89. 0	126. 0
14. 0	52. 0	90. 0	127. 0
15. 0	53. 0	91. 0	128. 0
16. 0	54. 0	92. 0	129. 0
17. 0	55. 0	93. 0	130. 0
18. 0	56. 0	94. 0	131. 12, 17
19. 0	57. 0	95. 0	132. 0
20. 0	58. 0	96. 0	133. 6
21. 0	59. 0	97. 0	134. 14
22. 0	60. 0	98. 0	135. 0
23. 0	61. 0	99. 0	136. 0
24. 0	62. 0	100. 0	137. 0
25. 0	63. 0	101. 0	138. 0
26. 0	64. 0	102. 0	139. 0
27. 0	65. 0	103. 0	140. 0
28. 0	66. 0	104. 0	141. 0
29. 0	67. 8	105. 0	142. 0
30. 0	68. 9	106. 0	143. 0
31. 0	69. 0	107. 0	144. 0
32. 0	70. 4	108. 0	145. 0
33. 0	71. 0	109. 0	146. 0
34. 0	72. 0	110. 0	147. 0
35. 0	73. 0	111. 0	148. 0
36. 0	74. 0	112. 0	149. 0
37. 0	75. 0	113. 0	150. 0
38. 0	76. 0		

K

1. 0	39. 0	77. 0	114. 0
2. 0	40. 14	78. 20	115. 0
3. 0	41. 0	79. 0	116. 0
4. 0	42. 0	80. 0	117. 24
5. 5	43. 6	81. 0	118. 0
6. 0	44. 4	82. 0	119. 13
7. 5	45. 0	83. 0	120. 0
8. 0	46. 0	84. 4	121. 0
9. 0	47. 0	85. 32	122. 0
10. 0	48. 0	86. 0	123. 3
11. 0	49. 0	87. 3	124. 0
12. 1	50. 0	88. 0	125. 0
13. 1, 17	51. 14	89. 0	126. 0
14. 0	52. 12	90. 0	127. 0
15. 0	53. 0	91. 0	128. 5
16. 0	54. 0	92. 4	129. 0
17. 0	55. 0	93. 13	130. 0
18. 0	56. 0	94. 0	131. 20
19. 0	57. 0	95. 0	132. 0
20. 5	58. 0	96. 0	133. 8
21. 0	59. 0	97. 0	134. 13, 17
22. 0	60. 5	98. 0	135. 0
23. 0	61. 11	99. 19	136. 1
24. 5	62. 0	100. 14, 20	137. 0
25. 0	63. 13	101. 0	138. 0
26. 0	64. 0	102. 0	139. 7, 12
27. 0	65. 0	103. 0	140. 0
28. 0	66. 0	104. 12	141. 0
29. 0	67. 0	105. 0	142. 0
30. 0	68. 0	106. 0	143. 0
31. 6	69. 0	107. 0	144. 0
32. 4	70. 13	108. 0	145. 0
33. 0	71. 0	109. 0	146. 0
34. 13	72. 5, 9	110. 8	147. 7
35. 13	73. 0	111. 0	148. 0
36. 0	74. 0	112. 0	149. 5
37. 0	75. 0	113. 0	150. 0
38. 9	76. 0		

L

1. 2
2. 12
3. 9
4. 0
5. 0
6. 3, 4
7. 2
8. 5, 9
9. 17
10. 3
11. 2
12. 0
13. 0
14. 4
15. 5, 10
16. 5
17. 14
18. 0
19. 20
20. 15
21. 0
22. 6, 11
23. 0
24. 8
25. 6
26. 13
27. 5
28. 8
29. 8
30. 0
31. 3
32. 0
33. 0
34. 1, 8, 11
35. 4
36. 9
37. 7
38. 13

39. 0
40. 16, 17
41. 2, 9
42. 0
43. 0
44. 0
45. 5, 11
46. 5, 26, 27
47. 0
48. 22, 23
49. 10, 18
50. 0
51. 0
52. 19
53. 17
54. 5, 12, 23
55. 0
56. 19
57. 0
58. 15, 16
59. 11
60. 0
61. 3
62. 14
63. 0
64. 14
65. 0
66. 0
67. 0
68. 13
69. 3, 13
70. 14
71. 0
72. 0
73. 5, 10, 15
74. 0
75. 0
76. 0

77. 0
78. 0
79. 0
80. 18
81. 14
82. 22
83. 13
84. 1
85. 1, 5
86. 0
87. 13
88. 14
89. 2, 18
90. 0
91. 7
92. 0
93. 0
94. 17
95. 13
96. 0
97. 0
98. 0
99. 9
100. 0
101. 19
102. 6
103. 18
104. 6
105. 0
106. 4, 13, 20, 21
107. 0
108. 8
109. 0
110. 5, 11
111. 0
112. 15, 23
113. 0

114. 3, 17
115. 0
116. 8
117. 0
118. 10, 11, 16
119. 0
120. 0
121. 0
122. 3, 16
123. 0
124. 5, 8
125. 0
126. 2, 14
127. 3, 17
128. 0
129. 12
130. 7
131. 0
132. 18
133. 0
134. 1, 10, 21
135. 1, 7, 8, 15
136. 0
137. 1, 12, 17
138. 1
139. 0
140. 0
141. 12
142. 3, 11
143. 3
144. 6
145. 3, 4
146. 6, 19
147. 0
148. 0
149. 6, 11, 22
150. 12

M

1. 18	39. 0	77. 3	114. 20
2. 0	40. 21	78. 1	115. 0
3. 0	41. 0	79. 4	116. 0
4. 0	42. 2, 10	80. 5, 12	117. 0
5. 12	43. 0	81. 0	118. 5
6. 7	44. 0	82. 0	119. 0
7. 0	45. 8	83. 16	120. 0
8. 10	46. 0	84. 16	121. 11
9. 7	47. 5	85. 0	122. 1
10. 0	48. 19	86. 0	123. 1, 9
11. 0	49. 0	87. 5	124. 0
12. 0	50. 9, 10, 14	88. 3	125. 0
13. 0	51. 7	89. 0	126. 0
14. 1	52. 3	90. 6	127. 0
15. 0	53. 0	91. 0	128. 17
16. 0	54. 0	92. 0	129. 3
17. 0	55. 0	93. 0	130. 0
18. 0	56. 0	94. 0	131. 0
19. 0	57. 0	95. 0	132. 0
20. 0	58. 0	96. 0	133. 0
21. 0	59. 0	97. 0	134. 0
22. 13	60. 0	98. 0	135. 0
23. 4	61. 0	99. 16	136. 0
24. 3	62. 0	100. 0	137. 0
25. 0	63. 0	101. 21	138. 13, 26
26. 0	64. 0	102. 0	139. 0
27. 0	65. 16	103. 12, 16	140. 0
28. 0	66. 0	104. 0	141. 0
29. 20	67. 1, 10	105. 0	142. 4
30. 15	68. 0	106. 0	143. 0
31. 9	69. 0	107. 1	144. 18
32. 17	70. 6	108. 1, 13, 18	145. 0
33. 0	71. 0	109. 9	146. 10
34. 0	72. 6	110. 12	147. 0
35. 0	73. 1	111. 0	148. 0
36. 5, 11	74. 0	112. 0	149. 0
37. 0	75. 0	113. 10	150. 0
38. 0	76. 16		

N

1. 6, 9, 15
2. 2, 7, 10, 16, 20
3. 3
4. 16
5. 10
6. 12
7. 0
8. 3
9. 15
10. 5, 13
11. 4, 9
12. 8, 16
13. 3, 12, 18
14. 0
15. 0
16. 3, 12
17. 0
18. 5, 18
19. 0
20. 0
21. 7
22. 0
23. 15
24. 10
25. 8, 13
26. 11, 18, 19
27. 7, 10
28. 0
29. 14
30. 17
31. 12, 14, 18, 23
32. 0
33. 0
34. 5
35. 0
36. 16
37. 3, 17
38. 0

39. 10
40. 9, 19
41. 0
42. 15, 21
43. 0
44. 6
45. 14
46. 13
47. 0
48. 6
49. 4, 14
50. 6, 12, 16
51. 16
52. 11, 13, 16
53. 0
54. 31
55. 11
56. 3
57. 6
58. 0
59. 6
60. 2
61. 10
62. 9
63. 6
64. 3, 16
65. 0
66. 2
67. 7, 13, 18
68. 0
69. 0
70. 3, 8, 12, 16
71. 16
72. 0
73. 12
74. 11, 16, 21
75. 3
76. 6

77. 0
78. 10
79. 15
80. 7, 10, 14
81. 5
82. 0
83. 18
84. 6, 14, 21
85. 12, 14, 15, 19
86. 8
87. 0
88. 6, 12, 19
89. 6, 9, 15
90. 15, 16
91. 15, 17, 22
92. 15
93. 0
94. 0
95. 21, 24
96. 10
97. 21, 23
98. 8
99. 2, 7, 18, 21
100. 0
101. 3
102. 8, 15, 19, 29
103. 5
104. 2
105. 11
106. 8
107. 7
108. 12
109. 11
110. 0
111. 8
112. 0

113. 7
114. 5, 9, 10, 15
115. 5
116. 5, 14
117. 6, 10
118. 7, 12
119. 6
120. 4, 12
121. 7, 13
122. 8
123. 5
124. 13
125. 2, 8
126. 5
127. 8, 19
128. 4, 19
129. 5, 7, 16
130. 3
131. 10, 23
132. 9, 16
133. 10, 14, 15
134. 0
135. 20
136. 3, 4, 15
137. 5, 8
138. 9, 15
139. 1, 18
140. 18
141. 10
142. 0
143. 6
144. 5, 14, 24
145. 0
146. 12
147. 0
148. 7
149. 4, 8, 13
150. 4, 8, 19

0

1. 13
2. 14, 22
3. 0
4. 18
5. 0
6. 0
7. 9
8. 4
9. 0
10. 0
11. 3, 15, 16
12. 0
13. 0
14. 5
15. 2, 11
16. 2, 9
17. 3, 7
18. 2, 3
19. 18
20. 6
21. 5, 6
22. 2, 9
23. 3, 10
24. 2, 9, 14, 19
25. 12
26. 0
27. 0
28. 11
29. 18
30. 0
31. 19, 22
32. 2, 7
33. 0
34. 2
35. 7, 11, 12
36. 4, 6
37. 16
38. 7
39. 0

40. 0
41. 12
42. 0
43. 4, 13
44. 2, 9
45. 0
46. 23
47. 15, 18
48. 2, 11, 15, 18, 21
49. 0
50. 8
51. 12
52. 2, 5, 14, 18
53. 5, 18
54. 2, 8, 20, 26
55. 10
56. 2, 18
57. 18, 25
58. 14
59. 0
60. 0
61. 9
62. 0
63. 5, 7, 14
64. 0
65. 5, 9, 13
66. 17
67. 0
68. 0
69. 6, 14
70. 0
71. 2, 7
72. 3
73. 2
74. 5, 8, 9
75. 5

76. 0
77. 0
78. 4, 24
79. 3, 14
80. 0
81. 11
82. 2, 12
83. 2, 14
84. 2, 0, 0, 12, 20
85. 7
86. 7, 10
87. 8, 10
88. 9, 11, 18
89. 3
90. 0
91. 6, 18
92. 2
93. 2
94. 8, 11, 15
95. 19
96. 3
97. 3, 22
98. 4, 7
99. 1, 14
100. 0
101. 5, 18
102. 4, 17, 28
103. 14
104. 21, 24
105. 0
106. 10, 19, 22
107. 0
108. 5, 7, 19
109. 2
110. 6, 10
111. 7, 12, 15
112. 2, 14
113. 0

114. 8, 14
115. 10
116. 0
117. 15
118. 13
119. 2, 5, 11
120. 0
121. 5, 9, 12, 21
122. 5
123. 8, 11, 15
124. 12
125. 19
126. 0
127. 9, 16
128. 0
129. 2
130. 0
131. 22
132. 2
133. 0
134. 0
135. 14, 22
136. 0
137. 15
138. 0
139. 5, 10
140. 3, 5, 15, 17
141. 6
142. 12
143. 2
144. 4, 17, 21
145. 8
146. 0
147. 15
148. 3, 17
149. 14, 16, 17
150. 18

P

1. 0	39. 0	77. 0	114. 0
2. 5, 23	40. 7	78. 0	115. 0
3. 13	41. 0	79. 0	116. 1
4. 0	42. 0	80. 0	117. 0
5. 0	43. 0	81. 0	118. 0
6. 0	44. 0	82. 10	119. 0
7. 12	45. 0	83. 1, 3	120. 0
8. 7	46. 0	84. 0	121. 0
9. 0	47. 0	85. 9	122. 0
10. 0	48. 0	86. 0	123. 0
11. 0	49. 0	87. 0	124. 11
12. 12	50. 0	88. 4	125. 18, 20
13. 0	51. 0	89. 0	126. 0
14. 0	52. 0	90. 0	127. 0
15. 0	53. 0	91. 0	128. 0
16. 0	54. 11	92. 10	129. 0
17. 10	55. 0	93. 0	130. 0
18. 15	56. 17	94. 0	131. 0
19. 14	57. 1	95. 10	132. 3, 6
20. 2	58. 8	96. 0	133. 1
21. 0	59. 8	97. 0	134. 0
22. 0	60. 6	98. 3	135. 0
23. 0	61. 0	99. 12	136. 9
24. 0	62. 0	100. 10	137. 14
25. 0	63. 0	101. 0	138. 7
26. 9	64. 0	102. 12, 13, 24	139. 0
27. 0	65. 0	103. 0	140. 10
28. 0	66. 16	104. 4, 5, 15	141. 4
29. 0	67. 11	105. 5	142. 1
30. 7	68. 0	106. 16	143. 0
31. 4	69. 7, 11	107. 0	144. 0
32. 0	70. 0	108. 0	145. 0
33. 0	71. 0	109. 13	146. 0
34. 0	72. 0	110. 0	147. 0
35. 0	73. 9	111. 0	148. 0
36. 0	74. 0	112. 0	149. 0
37. 8	75. 0	113. 13	150. 0
38. 0	76. 0		

Q

1. 0	39. 0	77. 0	114. 0
2. 0	40. 0	78. 0	115. 1
3. 0	41. 0	79. 0	116. 0
4. 0	42. 0	80. 0	117. 21
5. 0	43. 0	81. 0	118. 0
6. 0	44. 0	82. 0	119. 0
7. 0	45. 0	83. 0	120. 0
8. 0	46. 0	84. 0	121. 0
9. 0	47. 0	85. 0	122. 0
10. 0	48. 0	86. 0	123. 0
11. 0	49. 0	87. 0	124. 16
12. 0	50. 0	88. 0	125. 0
13. 0	51. 0	89. 0	126. 0
14. 0	52. 0	90. 0	127. 0
15. 0	53. 0	91. 0	128. 0
16. 0	54. 0	92. 0	129. 0
17. 0	55. 0	93. 0	130. 9
18. 0	56. 0	94. 0	131. 0
19. 0	57. 0	95. 0	132. 0
20. 0	58. 0	96. 0	133. 0
21. 0	59. 0	97. 0	134. 0
22. 0	60. 0	98. 0	135. 0
23. 0	61. 0	99. 0	136. 0
24. 0	62. 0	100. 0	137. 0
25. 0	63. 0	101. 0	138. 0
26. 0	64. 0	102. 0	139. 0
27. 0	65. 0	103. 0	140. 0
28. 1	66. 0	104. 0	141. 0
29. 0	67. 0	105. 0	142. 0
30. 0	68. 0	106. 0	143. 0
31. 0	69. 0	107. 0	144. 0
32. 0	70. 0	108. 0	145. 0
33. 0	71. 3	109. 0	146. 0
34. 0	72. 0	110. 0	147. 0
35. 0	73. 0	111. 0	148. 13
36. 0	74. 0	112. 0	149. 0
37. 0	75. 0	113. 0	150. 0
38. 0	76. 0		

R

1. 0
2. 25
3. 15
4. 21
5. 4, 6
6. 14
7. 16
8. 2, 12
9. 6, 12
10. 18
11. 0
12. 6, 15
13. 6, 10
14. 6, 9, 11
15. 4, 14
16. 15
17. 2, 8
18. 16
19. 3
20. 0
21. 3
22. 1
23. 2, 7, 14
24. 15, 20
25. 2
26. 7, 21
27. 0
28. 13
29. 19
30. 1, 6, 11
31. 1, 7, 20
32. 1, 6, 14
33. 7
34. 15
35. 3
36. 0
37. 5, 9, 19
38. 2

39. 13
40. 0
41. 13
42. 4, 5
43. 7
44. 1, 10
45. 4
46. 9, 24
47. 7, 11, 17
48. 13, 25
49. 22
50. 0
51. 3
52. 23
53. 0
54. 10, 17, 28
55. 3, 4, 6, 13
56. 0
57. 13, 19, 26
58. 0
59. 14
60. 7
61. 6, 8
62. 5
63. 3, 8
64. 13
65. 18
66. 14, 18, 21
67. 0
68. 4, 5
69. 10
70. 10
71. 1, 8, 11
72. 8, 13
73. 8
74. 0
75. 12
76. 18, 21

77. 2
78. 5, 17, 23
79. 12
80. 16
81. 0
82. 8, 11
83. 15
84. 13, 19
85. 8, 28
86. 3, 4, 11
87. 12, 18
88. 0
89. 4
90. 11, 18
91. 10, 31
92. 3, 8
93. 3, 10
94. 16
95. 3
96. 4, 9, 12
97. 10, 17
98. 10
99. 15
100. 2
101. 9, 11
102. 23, 26
103. 0
104. 25
105. 14
106. 0
107. 4
108. 4, 22
109. 8, 15
110. 4
111. 5
112. 1, 7, 9, 20
113. 6, 16

114. 2, 24
115. 11
116. 3
117. 8, 18
118. 0
119. 17
120. 0
121. 17
122. 7, 14
123. 12, 16
124. 14
125. 0
126. 0
127. 1, 10, 15
128. 2, 8, 16
129. 14, 19
130. 5
131. 4, 8
132. 7, 15
133. 0
134. 23
135. 0
136. 18
137. 21
138. 24
139. 6
140. 6, 11
141. 1
142. 13
143. 12
144. 0
145. 9
146. 0
147. 0
148. 2, 18
149. 2, 15
150. 2, 10

S

1. 12
2. 0
3. 5, 16
4. 14
5. 1
6. 8
7. 11
8. 0
9. 0
10. 19
11. 0
12. 0
13. 16, 23
14. 0
15. 0
16. 17
17. 4, 5
18. 10
19. 9, 13
20. 1
21. 9
22. 4
23. 0
24. 12, 17
25. 10
26. 4, 8
27. 1, 12
28. 0
29. 1, 10
30. 0
31. 0
32. 0
33. 0
34. 3, 10, 16
35. 5, 16
36. 0
37. 0
38. 0

39. 15
40. 4, 6, 10, 13
41. 6, 14, 16
42. 0
43. 15
44. 11
45. 1
46. 17
47. 13
48. 0
49. 1, 7
50. 18
51. 5, 9, 10
52. 17
53. 8, 14, 19
54. 15
55. 9
56. 5, 9, 15
57. 27
58. 0
59. 1, 7
60. 1
61. 0
62. 1
63. 0
64. 7
65. 7, 12
66. 5
67. 19
68. 8
69. 0
70. 0
71. 13, 14
72. 1, 15
73. 0
74. 14, 24
75. 9

76. 0
77. 11
78. 6
79. 6, 13
80. 8, 19
81. 3
82. 0
83. 10
84. 0
85. 33
86. 6
87. 0
88. 16, 20
89. 0
90. 0
91. 0
92. 5
93. 0
94. 6, 19
95. 0
96. 14
97. 8
98. 0
99. 0
100. 4, 6, 11, 16
101. 15
102. 27
103. 0
104. 16
105. 7
106. 12
107. 0
108. 15
109. 4
110. 1, 14
111. 14
112. 3, 5, 18

113. 3, 12
114. 0
115. 0
116. 17, 22
117. 4, 13
118. 18
119. 8, 9, 21
120. 1
121. 19
122. 12
123. 17
124. 19
125. 0
126. 7, 12
127. 0
128. 12
129. 20
130. 12
131. 14, 15, 21
132. 5, 11
133. 4
134. 3, 8
135. 4
136. 8
137. 0
138. 11
139. 8
140. 0
141. 5
142. 0
143. 0
144. 22
145. 0
146. 0
147. 22
148. 4, 5
149. 18
150. 13

T

1. 16
2. 11, 27
3. 0
4. 6
5. 2
6. 11
7. 0
8. 0
9. 1, 11
10. 2, 6, 11
11. 0
12. 3
13. 7, 22
14. 0
15. 0
16. 8, 13, 18
17. 0
18. 9, 14
19. 6, 10
20. 8
21. 4, 10
22. 5
23. 9, 12, 17
24. 1, 13, 21
25. 9, 11
26. 1, 5
27. 2, 8
28. 4
29. 5, 11
30. 9, 10, 14, 18
31. 21
32. 0
33. 4, 8, 14
34. 0
35. 9
36. 3
37. 12, 14
38. 5, 10
39. 1, 8

40. 1
41. 0
42. 0
43. 1
44. 0
45. 0
46. 3, 10, 18
47. 14
48. 9, 16, 17
49. 0
50. 1, 4, 17
51. 6, 11
52. 1, 7
53. 10, 12, 20
54. 0
55. 0
56. 6, 10, 16
57. 3, 4, 8, 14, 21
58. 10
59. 2
60. 0
61. 4, 13
62. 3, 13
63. 9, 15
64. 10
65. 1, 11
66. 6, 10, 19
67. 0
68. 0
69. 8, 15
70. 0
71. 9
72. 2, 11
73. 0
74. 0
75. 0
76. 3, 4, 14
77. 0
78. 11, 21

79. 1
80. 3
81. 6, 9, 13
82. 17
83. 7
84. 10
85. 3, 4
86. 0
87. 1, 7
88. 8
89. 13
90. 0
91. 1, 9, 12, 19, 26, 27, 30, 33
92. 0
93. 6
94. 1, 7, 12
95. 4, 22, 25
96. 0
97. 1, 14, 15, 18
98. 0
99. 8
100. 12, 17, 22
101. 13
102. 2, 9, 16
103. 7, 10
104. 17, 23
105. 8
106. 1
107. 0
108. 3, 10, 23
109. 16
110. 0
111. 10
112. 17
113. 4
114. 7, 12, 22
115. 9

116. 6
117. 1, 19
118. 8, 14
119. 10
120. 0
121. 1, 8, 14, 20
122. 13
123. 0
124. 20
125. 13, 15
126. 13
127. 11
128. 9, 13
129. 21
130. 4, 13
131. 1
132. 13
133. 3, 20
134. 0
135. 3, 9, 17
136. 16
137. 9
138. 3, 4, 16, 19, 20
139. 9
140. 1, 7
141. 0
142. 0
143. 9
144. 8, 9, 16, 20
145. 0
146. 1, 14
147. 1, 12, 17, 23
148. 9, 16
149. 23
150. 9, 14, 16

U

1. 0	39. 0	76. 17	114. 0
2. 0	40. 5	77. 6	115. 2
3. 0	41. 0	78. 25	116. 10, 18
4. 0	42. 0	79. 0	117. 22
5. 0	43. 0	80. 0	118. 0
6. 0	44. 0	81. 12	119. 0
7. 0	45. 0	82. 0	120. 0
8. 0	46. 16	83. 0	121. 6
9. 8	47. 0	84. 9, 15	122. 6, 11
10. 0	48. 3, 12	85. 30	123. 0
11. 0	49. 0	86. 0	124. 10, 17
12. 14	50. 0	87. 11	125. 4
13. 9	51. 0	88. 2, 15	126. 0
14. 0	52. 10	89. 0	127. 0
15. 3	53. 0	90. 0	128. 7
16. 0	54. 3, 9, 16,	91. 11, 25, 32	129. 0
17. 11	21, 27, 30	92. 11	130. 10
18. 0	55. 0	93. 0	131. 0
19. 0	56. 0	94. 0	132. 0
20. 0	57. 2	95. 11, 20	133. 0
21. 0	58. 0	96. 0	134. 0
22. 0	59. 0	97. 0	135. 0
23. 0	60. 0	98. 0	136. 0
24. 0	61. 0	99. 0	137. 18, 20
25. 0	62. 4	100. 0	138. 8
26. 0	63. 0	101. 6, 20	139. 0
27. 0	64. 0	102. 5	140. 0
28. 2, 12	65. 10	103. 0	141. 13
29. 0	66. 0	104. 0	142. 0
30. 0	67. 9	105. 2, 10	143. 0
31. 0	68. 10	106. 0	144. 10
32. 0	69. 0	107. 0	145. 0
33. 0	70. 0	108. 14, 17	146. 9
34. 0	71. 4	109. 3	147. 0
35. 8	72. 0	110. 0	148. 14
36. 2	73. 16	111. 0	149. 0
37. 0	74. 0	112. 24	150. 0
38. 3	75. 0	113. 0	

V

1. 0	39. 0	77. 0	114. 0
2. 0	40. 0	78. 0	115. 6
3. 0	41. 0	79. 0	116. 0
4. 9	42. 19	80. 1	117. 0
5. 8	43. 0	81. 17	118. 0
6. 0	44. 0	82. 1	119. 15
7. 0	45. 0	83. 0	120. 0
8. 0	46. 0	84. 0	121. 0
9. 0	47. 3	85. 0	122. 0
10. 0	48. 0	86. 0	123. 0
11. 0	49. 20	87. 0	124. 2
12. 0	50. 0	88. 0	125. 0
13. 0	51. 0	89. 0	126. 0
14. 0	52. 0	90. 0	127. 0
15. 12	53. 0	91. 0	128. 0
16. 0	54. 0	92. 0	129. 0
17. 0	55. 0	93. 0	130. 1
18. 0	56. 0	94. 0	131. 6
19. 1	57. 0	95. 0	132. 0
20. 13	58. 0	96. 0	133. 12
21. 0	59. 4	97. 0	134. 4
22. 0	60. 9	98. 0	135. 0
23. 0	61. 0	99. 0	136. 0
24. 0	62. 16	100. 0	137. 3
25. 0	63. 0	101. 1, 7	138. 0
26. 0	64. 5	102. 0	139. 0
27. 3	65. 0	103. 3	140. 0
28. 0	66. 3, 12	104. 0	141. 0
29. 3	67. 0	105. 0	142. 0
30. 0	68. 0	106. 0	143. 0
31. 0	69. 0	107. 0	144. 0
32. 0	70. 0	108. 0	145. 1
33. 0	71. 0	109. 0	146. 0
34. 0	72. 0	110. 0	147. 0
35. 0	73. 0	111. 0	148. 0
36. 0	74. 2	112. 12	149. 20
37. 0	75. 0	113. 0	150. 0
38. 0	76. 0		

W

1. 14	39. 0	77. 0	114. 0
2. 15	40. 0	78. 0	115. 0
3. 1, 11	41. 0	79. 0	116. 0
4. 2, 19	42. 0	80. 0	117. 0
5. 0	43. 0	81. 7	118. 0
6. 1	44. 0	82. 5, 24	119. 3
7. 6, 10	45. 0	83. 0	120. 0
8. 0	46. 1	84. 0	121. 0
9. 0	47. 21	85. 26	122. 0
10. 15	48. 0	86. 0	123. 0
11. 14	49. 0	87. 0	124. 0
12. 0	50. 0	88. 0	125. 11
13. 0	51. 0	89. 0	126. 9
14. 0	52. 15	90. 9, 13	127. 0
15. 0	53. 3	91. 4	128. 10
16. 0	54. 0	92. 0	129. 1
17. 6	55. 0	93. 0	130. 0
18. 11	56. 0	94. 14	131. 0
19. 0	57. 0	95. 0	132. 0
20. 0	58. 0	96. 17	133. 17
21. 0	59. 0	97. 2	134. 0
22. 0	60. 12	98. 0	135. 12
23. 0	61. 1	99. 0	136. 0
24. 0	62. 0	100. 7	137. 0
25. 0	63. 0	101. 0	138. 0
26. 0	64. 8	102. 0	139. 3
27. 0	65. 0	103. 0	140. 2
28. 5	66. 0	104. 27	141. 0
29. 0	67. 0	105. 0	142. 0
30. 0	68. 0	106. 23	143. 0
31. 0	69. 0	107. 0	144. 26
32. 0	70. 0	108. 0	145. 0
33. 0	71. 0	109. 6	146. 2
34. 0	72. 0	110. 0	147. 4, 10, 20
35. 0	73. 0	111. 0	148. 0
36. 0	74. 13, 23	112. 0	149. 0
37. 0	75. 1, 6, 7	113. 1	150. 0
38. 0	76. 9, 12		

X

1. 0	39. 0	77. 0	114. 0
2. 0	40. 0	78. 0	115. 0
3. 0	41. 0	79. 0	116. 0
4. 0	42. 0	80. 0	117. 0
5. 0	43. 0	81. 0	118. 0
6. 0	44. 0	82. 0	119. 0
7. 0	45. 0	83. 0	120. 0
8. 0	46. 0	84. 0	121. 0
9. 0	47. 0	85. 0	122. 0
10. 0	48. 0	86. 0	123. 0
11. 0	49. 0	87. 0	124. 0
12. 0	50. 0	88. 0	125. 0
13. 0	51. 0	89. 0	126. 0
14. 0	52. 0	90. 0	127. 0
15. 0	53. 0	91. 0	128. 0
16. 0	54. 0	92. 0	129. 0
17. 0	55. 0	93. 0	130. 0
18. 0	56. 0	94. 0	131. 0
19. 0	57. 0	95. 0	132. 0
20. 0	58. 0	96. 0	133. 0
21. 0	59. 0	97. 0	134. 0
22. 0	60. 0	98. 0	135. 0
23. 0	61. 0	99. 0	136. 0
24. 0	62. 0	100. 0	137. 19
25. 0	63. 0	101. 0	138. 0
26. 0	64. 0	102. 0	139. 14
27. 0	65. 0	103. 0	140. 0
28. 0	66. 0	104. 0	141. 0
29. 0	67. 3	105. 0	142. 0
30. 0	68. 0	106. 0	143. 0
31. 0	69. 0	107. 0	144. 0
32. 0	70. 0	108. 0	145. 0
33. 0	71. 0	109. 0	146. 0
34. 0	72. 0	110. 0	147. 0
35. 0	73. 0	111. 0	148. 0
36. 0	74. 0	112. 0	149. 0
37. 0	75. 0	113. 0	150. 0
38. 0	76. 0		

Y

1. 0	39. 0	77. 4	114. 25
2. 13	40. 0	78. 0	115. 0
3. 0	41. 3	79. 0	116. 0
4. 0	42. 0	80. 0	117. 0
5. 0	43. 14	81. 0	118. 0
6. 0	44. 0	82. 21	119. 0
7. 0	45. 7	83. 5	120. 0
8. 0	46. 11	84. 0	121. 0
9. 0	47. 6, 23	85. 25	122. 0
10. 12, 21	48. 1, 10	86. 0	123. 2
11. 0	49. 0	87. 9	124. 0
12. 0	50. 0	88. 0	125. 0
13. 0	51. 0	89. 0	126. 0
14. 0	52. 0	90. 7	127. 0
15. 0	53. 0	91. 0	128. 20
16. 0	54. 7, 25	92. 1	129. 0
17. 0	55. 5	93. 0	130. 0
18. 0	56. 7, 22	94. 0	131. 0
19. 7	57. 0	95. 0	132. 0
20. 0	58. 0	96. 0	133. 0
21. 0	59. 0	97. 0	134. 0
22. 0	60. 0	98. 2	135. 0
23. 18	61. 0	99. 0	136. 7
24. 16	62. 8	100. 0	137. 22
25. 0	63. 0	101. 0	138. 0
26. 0	64. 0	102. 0	139. 4
27. 15	65. 6	103. 17	140. 0
28. 10	66. 0	104. 11, 29	141. 8
29. 0	67. 0	105. 15	142. 0
30. 0	68. 0	106. 17	143. 0
31. 0	69. 0	107. 0	144. 0
32. 5	70. 0	108. 0	145. 6
33. 0	71. 0	109. 17	146. 0
34. 0	72. 0	110. 0	147. 0
35. 0	73. 0	111. 0	148. 0
36. 0	74. 0	112. 0	149. 0
37. 0	75. 0	113. 0	150. 0
38. 0	76. 11		

Z

1. 0	39. 0	77. 0	114. 0
2. 0	40. 0	78. 0	115. 0
3. 0	41. 0	79. 0	116. 0
4. 0	42. 0	80. 0	117. 0
5. 0	43. 0	81. 0	118. 0
6. 0	44. 0	82. 0	119. 0
7. 0	45. 0	83. 0	120. 0
8. 0	46. 0	84. 0	121. 0
9. 0	47. 0	85. 0	122. 0
10. 0	48. 0	86. 0	123. 0
11. 0	49. 0	87. 0	124. 0
12. 0	50. 0	88. 0	125. 0
13. 0	51. 0	89. 0	126. 0
14. 0	52. 0	90. 0	127. 0
15. 0	53. 0	91. 0	128. 0
16. 0	54. 0	92. 0	129. 0
17. 12, 13	55. 0	93. 1	130. 0
18. 0	56. 0	94. 0	131. 0
19. 0	57. 0	95. 0	132. 0
20. 0	58. 0	96. 0	133. 0
21. 0	59. 0	97. 0	134. 0
22. 0	60. 0	98. 0	135. 0
23. 0	61. 0	99. 0	136. 0
24. 0	62. 0	100. 0	137. 0
25. 0	63. 0	101. 0	138. 0
26. 0	64. 11	102. 0	139. 0
27. 0	65. 0	103. 0	140. 0
28. 0	66. 0	104. 0	141. 0
29. 0	67. 0	105. 0	142. 0
30. 0	68. 0	106. 0	143. 0
31. 0	69. 0	107. 0	144. 0
32. 0	70. 0	108. 0	145. 0
33. 0	71. 0	109. 0	146. 0
34. 0	72. 0	110. 0	147. 0
35. 0	73. 0	111. 0	148. 0
36. 0	74. 0	112. 0	149. 0
37. 0	75. 0	113. 0	150. 0
38. 0	76. 0		

LEVEL 1—ANSWERS

1. A LEGEND IN HIS OWN TIME
2. INDEPENDENTLY OWNED AND OPERATED
3. WINDSHIELD WIPERS
4. DWIGHT DAVID EISENHOWER
5. STARK RAVING MAD
6. WILLIAM SHATNER
7. BLACK WIDOW SPIDER
8. ARNOLD PALMER
9. THE BERMUDA TRIANGLE
10. ATLANTIC CITY NEW JERSEY
11. BLONDIE AND DAGWOOD
12. KATHARINE HEPBURN
13. KING ARTHUR AND HIS KNIGHTS
14. MAIL-ORDER BRIDE
15. FOUR-LEAF CLOVER
16. CONFLICT OF INTEREST
17. CROSSWORD PUZZLE
18. GOOD NIGHT SWEET PRINCE
19. VARIETY IS THE SPICE OF LIFE
20. SPEAK OF THE DEVIL
21. CARTOONIST
22. ROAST LEG OF LAMB
23. FROM HERE TO ETERNITY
24. TO MAKE A LONG STORY SHORT
25. FRED FLINTSTONE
26. THE STAR-SPANGLED BANNER
27. ST. VALENTINE'S DAY
28. QUIT WHILE YOU'RE AHEAD
29. SAVE THE LAST DANCE FOR ME
30. RED-CARPET TREATMENT
31. RALPH KRAMDEN AND ED NORTON
32. ROCKY ROAD ICE CREAM
33. GIFT CERTIFICATE
34. LOS ANGELES LAKERS

35. GIRL SCOUT COOKIES
36. AUTOMOBILE MECHANIC
37. GENERAL PRACTITIONER
38. FRUIT COCKTAIL
39. THE FIGHTING IRISH
40. THE SUSPENSE IS KILLING ME
41. CLYDESDALE HORSES
42. A MARRIAGE MADE IN HEAVEN
43. THE OAK RIDGE BOYS
44. ROCKING HORSE
45. SHIRLEY MACLAINE
46. WITH LIBERTY AND JUSTICE FOR ALL
47. GIVE MY REGARDS TO BROADWAY
48. YOU CAN BET YOUR BOTTOM DOLLAR
49. SIGNED SEALED AND DELIVERED
50. THE TEN COMMANDMENTS

LEVEL II—ANSWERS

51. CHRISTMAS STOCKING
52. TOMB OF THE UNKNOWN SOLDIER
53. HE WHO HESITATES IS LOST
54. DOUBLE YOUR PLEASURE DOUBLE YOUR FUN
55. HARRY REASONER
56. HONESTY IS THE BEST POLICY
57. PUTTING THE CART BEFORE THE HORSE
58. CABBAGE PATCH DOLL
59. STEVEN SPIELBERG
60. SNEAK PREVIEW
61. WALTER CRONKITE
62. SATURDAY NIGHT LIVE
63. FARGO NORTH DAKOTA
64. GENEVA SWITZERLAND
65. THE BOY SCOUTS OF AMERICA
66. INVESTIGATIVE REPORTER
67. MEXICAN JUMPING BEANS
68. CHERRIES JUBILEE
69. HELICOPTER PILOT
70. BENJAMIN FRANKLIN
71. ROQUEFORT DRESSING
72. STOCK MARKET CRASH

73. MODEL AIRPLANE GLUE
74. I'VE GOT GOOD NEWS AND BAD NEWS
75. WINDOW WASHER
76. GETTING AWAY WITH MURDER
77. ARMY BUDDIES
78. MAJOR SCIENTIFIC BREAKTHROUGH
79. THOMAS JEFFERSON
80. VITAMINS AND MINERALS
81. ABSENT WITHOUT LEAVE
82. VOID WHERE PROHIBITED BY LAW
83. POPEYE THE SAILOR MAN
84. LOOKING OUT FOR NUMBER ONE
85. LITTLE ORPHAN ANNIE AND DADDY WARBUCKS
86. HARRISON FORD
87. TAKE ME TO YOUR LEADER
88. JUMPING TO CONCLUSIONS
89. FLORENCE NIGHTINGALE
90. ACADEMY AWARD WINNER
91. THE WHOLE TRUTH AND NOTHING BUT THE TRUTH
92. YORKSHIRE PUDDING
93. ZORBA THE GREEK
94. THE BEST OF BOTH WORLDS
95. CERTIFIED PUBLIC ACCOUNTANT
96. GEORGE BERNARD SHAW
97. TWO HEADS ARE BETTER THAN ONE
98. HYPOCHONDRIAC
99. ONE GIANT LEAP FOR MANKIND
100. IRISH SWEEPSTAKES TICKET

LEVEL III—ANSWERS

101. VANCOUVER BRITISH COLUMBIA
102. IT COULDN'T HAPPEN TO A NICER PERSON
103. HAVING THE TIME OF MY LIFE
104. AN APPLE A DAY KEEPS THE DOCTOR AWAY
105. BUDAPEST HUNGARY
106. THE LEGEND OF SLEEPY HOLLOW
107. MIGRAINE HEADACHE
108. METROPOLITAN MUSEUM OF ART
109. HOUSEWARMING PARTY
110. SHERLOCK HOLMES
111. BICARBONATE OF SODA

112. ROSES ARE RED VIOLETS ARE BLUE
113. WESTERN HEMISPHERE
114. ARLINGTON NATIONAL CEMETERY
115. QUEEN VICTORIA
116. PARENTAL GUIDANCE SUGGESTED
117. THE SAN FRANCISCO EARTHQUAKE
118. DEAD MEN TELL NO TALES
119. DOW JONES STOCK AVERAGES
120. SHANGHAI CHINA
121. THE COUNT OF MONTE CRISTO
122. MELBOURNE AUSTRALIA
123. MY KINDOM FOR A HORSE
124. AVAILABLE UPON REQUEST
125. AN AUDIENCE WITH THE POPE
126. CLEAN AS A WHISTLE
127. RALEIGH NORTH CAROLINA
128. FRANKFURT WEST GERMANY
129. WOMEN AND CHILDREN FIRST
130. VENTRILOQUIST
131. THE REVEREND JESSE JACKSON
132. HOPE SPRINGS ETERNAL
133. PAT SAJAK AND VANNA WHITE
134. LAS VEGAS BLACKJACK DEALER
135. LET'S CALL THE WHOLE THING OFF
136. KENNEDY SPACE CENTER
137. LIVING IN THE LAP OF LUXURY
138. LET THE PUNISHMENT FIT THE CRIME
139. NEW YORK STOCK EXCHANGE
140. TWO FOR THE PRICE OF ONE
141. RHAPSODY IN BLUE
142. PALM BEACH FLORIDA
143. GOLDEN GATE BRIDGE
144. BACON LETTUCE AND TOMATO SANDWICH
145. VALLEY FORGE
146. TWEEELEDUM AND TWEEDLEDEE
147. THE WICKED WITCH OF THE WEST
148. CROSSING THE EQUATOR
149. FRANKLIN DELANO ROOSEVELT
150. GRAND CENTRAL STATION

ENTER BANTAM BOOKS'
OFFICIAL WHEEL OF FORTUNE PUZZLE BOOK SWEEPSTAKES

Official Rules:

1.) *No Purchase Is Necessary.* Enter by completing the Official Entry Form and solving the Wheel of Fortune "Bonus Round Sweepstakes" puzzle found on the Official Entry Form, and sending it to:

Bantam Books
OFFICIAL WHEEL OF FORTUNE PUZZLE BOOK SWEEPSTAKES
Department JB
666 Fifth Avenue
New York, New York 10103

For an extra copy of the Official Entry Form and unsolved word puzzle, send your request by December 31, 1987 with a self-addressed stamped envelope to the above address.

2.) *Prizes*

1 Grand Prize:	Three-day trip for two to Hollywood, California. Prize includes round-trip coach airfare on Eastern Airlines (from nearest city to winner's residence from which Eastern Airlines flies to Los Angeles), deluxe double-occupancy hotel accommodations for two nights, and, subject to mutual date availability, a visit to the Wheel of Fortune television studio set, and, if the winner meets eligibility requirements, the opportunity to test and an audition to appear on Wheel of Fortune!* (Approximate Retail Value: $1,437.00).
25 First Prizes:	An Official Wheel of Fortune watch. (Approximate Retail Value: $39.95).
50 Second Prizes:	A pre-selected assortment of 8-10 paperback books from Bantam Books. (Approximate Retail Value: $35.00).

3.) Sweepstakes begins on November 5, 1987. All completed entries must be received by Bantam no later than January 30, 1988. The winners will be chosen by random drawing from the correct completed entries on or about March 1, 1988 and will be announced and notified on or about April 30, 1988. If there are not enough correct entries received to award all prizes, then the remaining prizes will be awarded by random drawing. Winners have 30 days from date of notice in which to accept their prize award or an alternative winner will be chosen. Grand Prize trip must be taken by October 30, 1988. Entrants must be 13 or older and if a minor, must be accompanied on Grand Prize trip by a parent or legal guardian. Odds of winning depend on the number of correct entries received. Enter as often as you wish, but each entry must be mailed separately. Limit one prize per household, address or organization. No prize substitutions, mechanically reproduced entries, or transfers allowed. Bantam is not responsible for lost or misdirected entries.

4.) Winners may be required to execute an Affidavit of Eligibility and Promotional Release supplied by Bantam. Entering the sweepstakes constitutes permission for use of winner's name, likeness and entry for publicity and promotional purposes, with no additional compensation.

5.) Employees of Bantam Doubleday Dell Publishing Group, Inc., Merv Griffin Enterprises, Sharp, International, and SpringGreen Marketing, their subsidiaries and affiliates, and their immediate family members are not eligible to enter this sweepstakes. This sweepstakes is open to residents of the U.S. and Canada, excluding the Province of Quebec. Void where prohibited or restricted by law. All federal, state and local regulations apply. Taxes, if any, are the winner's sole responsibility. If the winner is a minor, prize will be awarded in name of parent or guardian.

6.) For a list of major prize winner(s), send a stamped, self-addressed envelope entirely separate from your entry to Bantam Books' Official Wheel of Fortune Puzzle Book Sweepstakes Winners List, Bantam Books, 666 Fifth Avenue, Dept. JB-L, New York, New York 10103.

*(Subject to producer's determination.)

★ ★ ★ BONUS ROUND SWEEPSTAKES ★ ★ ★

CATEGORY: PHRASE

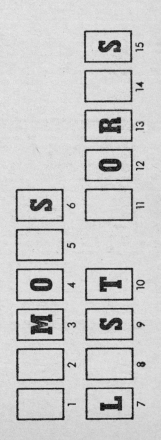

		M	O		S
1	2	3	4	5	6

L		S	T		
7	8	9	10	11	

	O	R		S
11	12	13	14	15

USED LETTER BOARD: R   S   T   L   M   O

(Remember to fill out Official Entry Form on reverse side.)

Bantam Books' Official Wheel of Fortune Puzzle Book Sweepstakes

OFFICIAL ENTRY FORM

Name _____

Address _____

City _____ State _____ Zip _____

Telephone No. _____

Age _____

Grand prize winners will enjoy the dynamic surroundings and proximity to Los Angeles attractions at the Westin Bonaventure—Landmark of Los Angeles.